LIGHTNING FO...

RAF Units 1960-1988 · A photographic appreciation of the English Electric Lightning

DALRYMPLE
& VERDUN◆
PUBLISHING

Front cover: Armed with fin-less drill rounds port side and an acquisition round on the starboard side, a pair of 5 Squadron's F Mk 6s, XS927/G and XR752/H return to a misty Leconfield from a June 1976 sortie.

Previous page: 74 Squadron show off their Lightning F Mk 1s at Coltishall in the early 1960s while a SAR Whirlwind hovers in the background.
via Martyn Chorlton

Left: WG763 the second P.1A at Warton pictured before its first flight which was on the 18th July 1955. *NWHG Warton*

Back cover: Busy scene at Wattisham on the 10th June 1963. The ASP is covered with Lightning F Mk 1As of 56 and 111 Squadron plus eight Javelin FAW Mk 8s of 41 Squadron.
via Martyn Chorlton

CONTENTS

Lightning Force
RAF Units 1960-1988, A photographic appreciation of the English Electric Lightning.
Fred Martin © 2005

ISBN 1- 905414-00-5

First published in 2005 by Dalrymple & Verdun Publishing, 33 Adelaide Street, Stamford, Lincolnshire, PE9 2EN England.
Tel: 0845 838 1940
E-mail: info@dvpublishing.co.uk

Design concept and layout © Dalrymple & Verdun Publishing and Stephen Thompson Associates.

All photographs by Fred Martin unless otherwise stated.

Printed in England by Ian Allan Printing Ltd
Riverdene Business Park, Molesey Road
Hersham, Surrey, KT12 4RG

All 13 of 111 Squadron's aircraft led by
George Black photographed in September
1965. *via George Black*

To this very day, and for many years to come, the Lightning fighter aircraft will continue to hold the imagination of young and old alike. Indeed, for many who were too young to remember the final days of this superb all-British supersonic fighter are equally enthused by the outstanding performance which was repeatedly demonstrated throughout its operational life of almost 30 years in frontline service. Interestingly, it has taken at least another generation of fighter aircraft before we are once more seeing the high agility and excellent thrust to weight performance ratio in Eurofighter/Typhoon which the Lightning demonstrated from its inception in the late fifties and early sixties.

Clearly, there was little else in any inventory of the worlds' air forces that could match its superior performance and handling qualities.

Reflecting back on my own experiences in the early days of squadron service it was clear from the outset that the aircraft was always to be a pilot's aeroplane. The same cannot be said for the engineering aspects of maintaining airworthiness of the fleet which throughout its service life posed a series of major challenges and heavy demands on the most resilient of engineering teams. In a word, the ratio of flying hours to the essential engineering effort was many times greater than the average for Royal Air Force aircraft at the time. The operational requirement of achieving and maintaining high readiness rates on a twenty four hour basis resulted in a necessity to work many long hours burning the midnight oil to ensure the daily task was met without shortfalls in serviceability. I have always believed that insufficient credit and recognition was given to this aspect of the aircraft and the tireless dedication needed to maintain its operational capability. I was privileged to be associated with the aircraft for over 15 years, initially as a squadron pilot on the newly formed 74 Squadron, then as OC of 111 Squadron followed by Chief Instructor/CFS Agent at the Lightning Operational Conversion Unit, before finally being OC 5 Squadron. All of which gave me a unique experience and opportunity to witness operations at the sharp-end but also

to fly almost all marks of the aircraft including the Royal Saudi Air Force T 55's which were based at RAF Coltishall for 18 months prior to deployment to the Kingdom of Saudi Arabia.

Over this period it was fortunate to be closely involved with the many and varied developments that both the aircraft and the operational role underwent, primarily necessitated by changes in the threat or to adapt to new theatres of operation. From the very early days of short-range UK Air Defence to the important impact of air-to-air refuelling, which greatly increased airborne time. But perhaps of greatest significance was the ability to expand the operational roles by deploying to new theatres of operation around the world. Similarly, on the home front it allowed interceptions to take place at much greater range from the UK than had previously been possible. Likewise, as the threat changed from one predominately at high altitude to one at low altitude, the Lightning had to be capable of covering the full spectrum of target heights from the very low to the very high. This posed new challenges for both the pilot and aircraft, to say little of the need to expand the training programme with new and complex flight profiles.

This book will revive many special and unique memories for its reader as well as the many enthusiasts who will revel in the detail of the various Squadrons who operated the aircraft. It will also provide a further useful edition to the historical record of this outstanding all-British fighter aircraft which was the first to exceed the speed of sound in level flight and perhaps more uniquely, break the sound barrier in a climb!

Lightning Force is a fine tribute to a remarkable fighter aircraft which by any standard was well ahead of its day in terms of performance and capability. It is also a fitting recognition to all the Royal Air Force men and women who served on Lightning squadrons and whose dedication achieved so much throughout the peak period of the Cold War. This book provides a remarkable photographic insight into the memorable era of the Lightning supersonic fighter, the finest, although sadly the last to be built in Britain.

George Black
Air Vice Marshal, RAF Retired,
June 2005

Converting from the Hunter F Mk 6 began in May 1960, with staff from the Lightning Conversion Unit (LCU) at Coltishall. This included seven days of ground instruction and ten one-hour sorties in the Lightning Mk 1 simulator, there being no two seat Lightnings available at the time.

The squadron's first Lightning F Mk 1 XM165, was delivered to Leconfield on 29th June 1960 as Coltishall's runways were under repair. It was ferried to its new owners by the Air Fighting Development Squadron (AFDS) on 11th July. The squadron's inaugural flight, in the hands of CO Sqn Ldr J F G Howe, took place on 14th July 1960 but the build up of aircraft was slow with only seven aircraft having been received by the end of August 1960.

flown to Boscombe Down on 1st September 1960 from where four Lightnings flew a four-ship formation at the Society of British Aerospace Companies Farnborough Air Show on all but one of the public days. Appearances were also made for the annual 'Battle of Britain at Home Day' air shows at RAF Waddington, Cottesmore, Wattisham, Biggin Hill, Gaydon and Bassingbourn, with a five-ship formation closing the show at Coltishall.

The chronic spares shortage improved significantly in December, pending a three-day publicity exercise to be staged at Coltishall in February 1961. No.74 Squadron was declared fully operational at the end of April 1961. The following month saw the squadron's involvement in their first exercise 'Matador' since re-equipping with the Lightning, at which they claimed twenty six 'kills' from nineteen sorties flown.

May also saw the squadron's return to formation flying for the 1961 air show season, beginning with a display at the Paris Air Salon in June and ending with a nine-ship team for the SBAC Farnborough show in September. Serviceability problems with the hydraulic system in January 1962 saw five aircraft in the hangar for modifications, whilst a further seven were undergoing various stages of their 200 hours service, leaving the squadron severely depleted of aircraft. They began to be returned to the squadron in April 1962 not to resume operational training but to provide Fighter Command's aerobatic team for the 1962 air show season. Beginning with a goodwill visit to Sweden and Norway in May, the highlight of the season's display activities was a synchronised formation of seven Lightnings and sixteen Hunters of No.92 Squadron 'The Blue Diamonds' at Farnborough in September. Prior to their Farnborough appearance the squadron's aircraft had their distinct black fin and spine livery applied. A display at Coltishall on 15th September 1962 marked the end of No.74 Squadron's official display commitments and return to its intended role.

1963 was the first year since re-equipping with the Lightning, that the squadron was fully occupied with operational training interspersed with the annual round of exercises, the most significant were 'Tophat' and 'Mystic', being held in July. The squadron lost its first aircraft XM142 on 26th April 1963, following a hydraulic failure. The pilot, Flt Lt Jim Burns, ejected successfully.

Following a move north to RAF Leuchars in Scotland on 28th January 1965 the squadron became the first to receive the Lightning F Mk 3, with the arrival of XP700 on 14th April. In June the squadron was declared temporarily non-operational whilst it was tasked with conducting intensive flight trials on the Lightning F Mk 3. The object of the trials being to rack up 300 hours on

74 SQUADRON

One of the Royal Air Force's most famous fighter squadrons, No.74 was selected to introduce Britain's first supersonic interceptor into service.

Pilot training continued unabated regardless of the number of aircraft available and most 'first solos' were accompanied by an instructor flying in a Hunter T Mk 7 to give practical and moral support by radio when required. It would still be three more years before the two seat Lightning T Mk 4 materialised. Low rate aircraft serviceability, which was an experience shared with almost all of the Lightning squadrons during their transition to the type, hindered operations with, on occasions, only one aircraft being available for flying at any given time. The major problems being a shortage of servicing equipment, spare parts and experienced technicians, to which was later added major hydraulic faults, poor radar serviceability and a number of spurious fire warning lights all of which required lengthy investigations and rectification. Nonetheless, to demonstrate the capabilities of the Lightning to the media and public alike, No.74 Squadron was directed to prepare for the first of a series of prestige commitments that would take precedence over operational training. With the squadron still well short of its full complement, six aircraft were each of eight aircraft so that an accurate assessment of component serviceability and servicing schedules could be made.

By April 1965 the squadron were involved in the first in-flight refuelling (IFR) trials, courtesy of the USAF and their KC-135s, as the RAF's own Valiant tankers had been permanently grounded due to severe fatigue problems. With the Victor tankers now coming on line, eight of No.74 Squadron's F Mk 3s were deployed to Cyprus during August and September 1965, with four of their number sent to Iran to stage a display to commemorate the Shah's birthday.

Continuing an annual event that was first hosted by No.74 Squadron in 1961, as a social meeting-cum-exercise amongst NATO squadrons whose emblem included a 'tiger', No.74 Squadron also hosted the last 'Tiger Meet' at Leuchars, between 5th and 9th July 1966.

No.74 Squadron then became the first to be equipped with the ultimate long range Lightning, the F Mk 6, with the arrival of XR768 at Leuchars on 1st August 1966. Being up to full strength by the end of the year, it was announced that the squadron was to be deployed to Singapore to become the air defence element of the Far East Air Force (FEAF). Operation 'Hydraulic', the deployment of the squadron's thirteen Lightning F Mk 6s began on the 4th June 1967. The aircraft staged through Akrotiri, Masirah and Gan, supported by Victor tankers of No.55, 57 and 214 Squadrons. This was the longest in-flight refuelling operation mounted by the RAF to date and the furthest distance a Lightning had flown.

Whilst in the Far East No.74 Squadron took part in a number of Air Defence exercises, the most notable ones being 'Town House' on 16th June 1969, when four F Mk 6s flew to Darwin in Northern Australia, and 'Bersatu Padu', which was a five-nation exercise held in August 1970 to test the air defences of Singapore Island and Western Malaya.

With the withdrawal of British Forces from the Far East No.74 Squadron disbanded on 1st September 1971. After four years of overseas service, the squadron's last task was to ferry its aircraft to Cyprus where they were used by No.56 Squadron as replacements for their Lightning F Mk 3s.

Below: Coltishall February 1961, with 74 Squadron lined up for presentation to the world's press. *NWHG Warton*

74 SQUADRON

Previously flew:
Hawker Hunter F Mk 6s since November 1957.

Lightnings:
F Mk 1s from 29th June 1960.
F Mk 3s from 14th April 1965.
F Mk 6s from 1st August 1966.

Bases:
Coltishall, Norfolk.
Leuchars, Scotland from 28th January 1965.
Tengah, Singapore from 4th June 1967.

Disbanded:
1st September 1971.

Later:
Reformed October 1974. Finally disbanded 22nd September 2000 as part of 4 Flying Training School, Valley, Wales, on BAe Hawk T Mk 1As.

Badge:
A tiger's face. Motto: I fear no man.

With engines running, No.74 Squadron's new Lightning F Mk 1s prepare to taxi out, 'to impress the press!' At the time, the Lightning F Mk 1 was undoubtedly the most impressive of the world's first generation of supersonic jet fighters and prestige commitments were given almost as much importance as operational requirements. Identifiable airframes include XM143/A, XM142/B, XM139/C and XM141/D. NWHG Warton

Impressive view of the first production variant, the Lightning F Mk 1, in this instance XM139/C, which displays its superbly uncluttered lines. The aircraft's primary armament of two de Havilland Firestreak infra-red, air-to-air, homing missiles was supplemented by two nose-mounted 30mm ADEN cannon. An additional pair of 30mm cannon could be carried under the fuselage as an alternative to the missile pack. The blanked-off lower gun port panels are visible in this photograph. NWHG Warton

Opposite page: With only seven Lightnings delivered by the end of August 1960, the squadron was tasked with providing a four aircraft display at that year's SBAC Farnborough Air Show at the beginning of September. By the end of the month a formation of five made an appearance at several RAF stations during the annual 'Battle of Britain At Home weekend'. Shown here are XM165/F, XM141/D, XM164/K, XM140/M and XM142/B. NWHG Warton

Based at Leuchars from 28th February 1964, No.74 Squadron became the first unit to equip with the new Lightning F Mk 3, receiving their first aircraft XP700 on 14th April 1964. Seen here are XP702/C and XP751/B in the sky over Leuchars. They both feature the black painted, square-topped, fin and have Firestreak infra-red, air-to-air, homing missiles fitted. *MoD*

Prior to delivery, XM145/Q was victim of a reheat fire during a ground run at Warton and subsequently was not received by No.74 Squadron until May 1962. This dramatic photograph was taken at Warton in 1963 prior to its delivery to the then Coltishall-based squadron. XM145 went on to serve with No.226 OCU and finally the Leuchars TFF until the end of 1970, before being scrapped after only 876 flying hours. In this photograph it does not have the ventral belly tank installed.
NWHG Warton

Photographed at Leuchars, F Mk 3 XP703/G and squadron companions share the ramp with the co-located No.23 Squadron which can be seen to the right in the background circa 1965. The Lightning F Mk 3 variant did not carry the internal 30mm cannon armament, but could support both Firestreak and the more capable Red Top, infra-red, air-to-air, homing missiles, which in the case of the latter was actually not to be until the squadron converted to the F Mk 6. The fin flash has been re-positioned and is angled parallel to the leading edge of the black-painted, square-topped, fin.

Whilst most of the country stayed at home to watch the legendary 1966 World Cup Final, the few who attended Leconfield's Open Day were rewarded with a splendid display given by XP706/L – in appaling weather. Having had their famous black fin and spine colours removed as part of the toning-down policy of the previous year, No.74 Squadron managed to retain a little colour by applying the squadron's black and yellow diced markings on their re-fuelling booms.

No.74 Squadron re-equipped with full standard Lightning F Mk 6s commencing 1st August 1966 and began a much travelled existence with numerous overseas deployments, including a courtesy visit to Iran. On 4th June 1967 the squadron started its move to the Far East Air Force to replace the Gloster Javelins of No.64 Squadron at Tengah, Singapore to become the air defence element at this far flung RAF outpost. XR768/A, (in the foreground), and companions are believed to be on the island of Gan on the outbound journey code-named 'Hydraulic'. This was the RAF's farthest air-to-air refuelling deployment to date.

No.74 Squadron's tenure at Tengah was to last until 25th August 1971, this being the squadron's last flying day. Whilst one Lightning F Mk 6 'holds' on Tengah's runway, another taxis out. Ground crews, some with cameras in hand, send off No.74 Squadron for a final ten-ship farewell formation flight from this FEAF base. *S J Bond*

56 SQUADRON

Flying Hunter F Mk 6s from Wattisham,

No.56 Squadron began to prepare for the conversion

to the Lightning in June 1960.

No.56 Squadron's first aircraft XM172 arrived on 14th December 1960 in the shape of the improved F Mk 1A variant, distinguished by its external cable ducting down the fuselage sides and by being 'plumbed' for in-flight refuelling.

The squadrons full complement, XM172-183 inclusive, had been received by March 1961. To assist in the work-up period a number of Hunters were retained and used as 'targets' during the early phase of radar training. As with No.74 Squadron, and indeed all Lightning squadrons, spares shortages and intensive servicing due to hydraulic and radar problems took their toll on serviceability.

But nevertheless, the squadron was declared fully operational on 14th July 1961, despite a prohibition on the use of the 30mm ADEN cannon and the aircraft's primary armament, the de Havilland Firestreak air-to-air homing missile, which at this time was still unproven. At the same time No.56 Squadron and their new aircraft were presented to the press with no effort being wasted, or lost, to demonstrate the capabilities of Britain's first supersonic fighter.

During September 1961, when another possible Berlin Crisis was in the making, No.56 Squadron detached six of their Lightnings on the 18th to Brüggen in what was then known as West Germany. Three pairs were flown at low level to attract as much attention as possible, with one pair, flying supersonic and practiced interceptions close to the Iron Curtain. Recovering to Brüggen, the aircraft were re-fuelled and returned home the same day from this, the first Lighting detachment to Germany.

Flight refuelling probes began to be delivered to the squadron in November 1961, but due to the Lightnings having a refit of their hydraulic systems by a contractor's working party, they were declared non-operational, thus training

did not begin until the following April, with the assistance of the 20th TFW/55th TFS and their F-100F's. The Super Sabre's in-flight refuelling probe was very similar to that of the Lightning, although mounted on the starboard wing (the opposite side to a Lightning), however valuable experience was gained.

The squadron made their first 'wet' hook-up with a Valiant tanker on 13th June and with their Lightnings beginning to be returned to them, intensive air refuelling trials began which would also test the aircraft's systems on long flights. With the success of the trials two Lightnings supported by five Valiant tankers deployed to Akrotiri, Cyprus on 23rd July 1962 in a four hour twenty minute flight. Four more aircraft followed in October but a planned detachment of the entire squadron was curtailed by a shortage of the single refuelling-point Valiant tankers. However, the ability to be able to deploy the RAF's premier interceptor had been demonstrated to all interested parties.

No.56 Squadron was selected to become Fighter Command's Lightning aerobatic team, taking over the mantle from No.74 Squadron. The New Year of 1963 began with close formation flying, between periods of Quick Reaction Alert (QRA) duty. A spectacular colour scheme was devised for their high profile aerobatic team role of a scarlet fin and spine quickly followed by the addition of red leading edges to the flying surfaces. Titled 'The Firebirds' (the name derived from its squadron badge) the squadron was unique amongst the Lightning teams as being the only one to generate smoke as part of the display. The season ended with a display at their home base of Wattisham in September 1963 and they then returned to operational duties.

With a deterioration of the political situation in Cyprus in 1964, a detachment of nine Lightnings was sent to Akrotiri on 6th February. Although a number of scrambles were ordered, only one successful interception took place, on two Turkish Air Force F-84 Thunderstreaks. The squadron began its return to Wattisham on 27th February 1965.

In March 1965, No.56 Squadron began to receive the new Lightning F Mk 3, with the old F Mk 1A's being stripped of their colourful paintwork and re-distributed to No.226 Operational Conversion Unit (OCU) and the Target Facilities Flights (TFF). With the F Mk 3 a new, even more spectacular, colour scheme was devised with the entire fin covered with the squadron's red and white checks, a red spine, and the squadron's badge placed within a new 'arrowhead' nose marking. Noticeable was the absence of the red, white and blue fin flash and the placement of the aircraft's individual letter on the airbrake doors. Not finding favour in 'high places', this scheme was instrumental in all of Fighter Command's aircraft being toned down in 1966, to a 'standardised scheme' of rectangular nose bars with the squadron's badge displayed on the fin within an 18 inch diameter white disc.

During October 1966, the squadron participated in the Malta Air Defence Exercise, taking with them five Lightning F Mk 3s and the T Mk 5. In February 1967 it was announced that No.56 Squadron would replace No.29 Squadron and their Javelins as the Near East Air Force's (NEAF) all-weather fighter defence force for the Sovereign Base Area of Cyprus. Now Red Top capable, the squadron began their deployment to Akrotiri in mid-April and were declared fully operational on 11th May. The end of this year proved to be a very busy period of QRA activity with a threatened Turkish invasion of the island.

As with the other Lightning squadrons, No.56 received a pair of Target Facilities Flight aircraft in the shape of two Canberras B Mk 2, WH666 and T Mk 4 WH861. The Lightning

Below: 'The Firebirds', with XM179 in the foreground prepare to depart a rather wet Wattisham for a practice display. *NWHG Warton*

F Mk 3s continued to serve until the arrival of the F Mk 6 in September 1971 and these aircraft were delivered by the now disbanded, UK bound, No.74 Squadron. These longer range aircraft improved the squadron's operational capabilities in the protection of the Sovereign Base Areas and were particularly put to the test in 1974, when over 200 operational sorties were flown as Turkish forces invaded the north of Cyprus.

With the withdrawal of RAF units from the island in January 1975, No.56 Squadron returned to Wattisham from where they operated with a mixed fleet of nine Lightning F Mk 6s, two F Mk 3s and a T Mk 5. Disbanded as a Lightning squadron on 28th June 1976, its aircraft were passed on to the Binbrook Wing and its 'number plate' was taken over by a newly formed Phantom FGR Mk 2 squadron at RAF Coningsby.

56 SQUADRON

Previously flew:
Hawker Hunter F Mk 6s since November 1958.

Lightnings:
F Mk 1As from 14th December 1960.
F Mk 3s from March 1965.
F Mk 6s from September 1971.

Bases:
Wattisham, Suffolk.
Akrotiri, Cyprus from 11th May 1967.
Wattisham, Suffolk from 21st January 1975.

Disbanded:
28th June 1976.

Later:
Reformed 30th June 1975 with McDonnell Douglas Phantom FGR Mk 2s. Currently flying Panavia Tornado F Mk 3s from Leuchars, Scotland.

Badge:
A phoenix amid flames.
Name: 'Punjab'
Motto: Quid si coelum ruat - What if heaven falls?

In 1963 'The Firebirds' took over the mantle of Fighter Command's aerobatic team from No.74 Squadron and decorated its Lightning F Mk 1s accordingly - probably the most colourful of all Lightning schemes, beautifully illustrated by XM171/A. To enable the team to trail smoke during their display routine, the port flap tank was modified to contain 33 gallons of diesel which was then pumped through piping routed through the starboard fuselage side and then injected behind the lower jet pipe. This produced a maximum three minutes of smoke. Only white smoke was used, another Lightning economy measure. *B Allchin*

The ability of the F Mk 1A to be air refuelled was soon exploited by the squadron. Here, XM172/S, the first of 56 Squadron Lightnings to be delivered, is seen taking on fuel from a Valiant tanker. *NWHG Warton*

Formation flying in jet fighters does not come much better than this. Eight F Mk 1A aircraft with the T Mk 4 in the centre put on a display for the camera in 1963. In common with other F Mk 1A aircraft at this time, the nose guns were removed but, uniquely to No.56 Squadron, so was the AI 23 radar which was replaced by lead weights. *NWHG Warton*

In June 1965, No.56 Squadron transitioned to the Lightning F Mk 3 variant and immediately adorned its Lightnings in this striking scheme, illustrated by XR718/C, which was devised by the squadron's Commander, Sqn Ldr I R 'Hank' Martin. To avoid disrupting the fin design, the fin flash has been omitted and the aircraft code letter placed on the air brake door. *B Allchin*

Above: A superb five ship formation of Lightning F Mk 3s in echelon to starboard. This stunning red and white check scheme was considered to be too outlandish by higher authority who subsequently initiated a general toning-down policy for all Fighter Command aircraft to a more standardised scheme. *B Allchin*

Opposite page top: No.56 Squadron moved to Akrotiri, Cyprus in April 1967, to take over the air defence responsibility of the island from No.29 Squadron and their Javelins. The squadron converted on to ex-No.74 Squadron F Mk 6s in the autumn of 1971. XS901/T was from a detachment of No.56 Squadron's Lightning F Mk 6s operating out of Binbrook in June 1972, on a Missile Practice Camp, whilst RAF Valley's runways were being repaired at the time. The white painted area on the dorsal spine is to reflect heat from the AVPIN tanks beneath.

Opposite page bottom: Turning sharply to avoid flying over the old market town of Beverley, situated at the south end of the runway, F Mk 6 XR759/P departs RAF Leconfield on a rather dismal day in July 1973, following the return of No.56 squadron to home soil for an Armament Practice Camp. The unit was operating out of both RAF Valley and RAF Leconfield.

Another view of F Mk 6 XR759/P during the July 1973 Armament Practice Camp. During the two week detachment, overwing tanks remained fitted to the aircraft. As usual the Red Top infra-red, air-to-air, homing missiles are fitted. The overwing tanks were painted Light Aircraft Grey around this time.

In common with the other F Mk 6 users, No.56 Squadron operated a couple of Lightning F Mk 3s in both operational and target facility roles. XP702/U was photographed at Coningsby in August 1975.

Opposite page: F Mk 6 XR773/N burns off excess fuel with a series of overshoots at Leconfield on its return from an APC sortie in June 1973. After later service with the Binbrook Wing, this particular aircraft replaced XR724 at Warton on Tornado trials before being transported to South Africa to fly again on 1st November 2001 at Thunder City, South Africa.

Opposite page top: The last Lightning T Mk 5 operated by No.56 squadron, XS417/Z, was photographed, in February 1975, visiting No.60 MU Leconfield whilst being used as a 'crew ferry'. *D Hemingway*

Opposite page bottom: With the withdrawal of RAF units from Cyprus in January 1975, No.56 Squadron returned to their former base at Wattisham. This particular Lightning F Mk 6, XS897/S, on the unit's strength at the time, was photographed at Lakenheath's 1975 Open House.

No.56 Squadron disbanded as a Lightning squadron on 28th June 1976. For eventual onward transfer to the Binbrook Wing, several F Mk 6s, including XR761/A seen here, were delivered to No.60 MU Leconfield. *D Hemingway*

XS919/R arrived at Leconfield from No. 56 Squadron at the end of 1975 for major servicing by No.60 MU. It is in fact seen here being returned to its hangar after engine runs in the spring of 1976. XS919 was later transferred to the Binbrook Wing.

Delivery was slow with the squadron literally waiting for the aircraft to be built, and it was not until 29th August 1961 with the arrival of XM216, the last F Mk 1A built, that the full complement was achieved. Typically, a serious shortage of servicing facilities and radar problems hindered the flying programme during the initial work up period, however the squadron was declared fully operational on 29th September 1961.

From April 1962, the squadron began to lose its aircraft to the hangar floor for a hydraulic re-work programme and it was not until July that the first aircraft became operational again. The slow return to operational status was somewhat alleviated by the delivery of the squadron's first Lightning T Mk 4 XM992 in September by which time only five Lightning F Mk 1A's had been recovered from the rework programme.

111 SQUADRON

With the delivery of Lightning F Mk 1A, XM185, to Wattisham on 6th March 1961, No.111 Squadron became the third and final operator of the first Lightning variant, sharing its base with the similarly equipped No.56 Squadron.

In October 1962, the Lightnings were again returned to the hangar, this time to be equipped with their in-flight refuelling probes, which would soon be put to full use with several overseas deployments over the coming years. Between 11th-17th November 1962, one of the squadron's aircraft, XM191, was involved in high-altitude interception trials, which included a successful sortie against a high flying USAF/CIA Lockheed U-2, much to the consternation of the Americans. In-flight refuelling training began in earnest in 1963 with a four aircraft deployment to Cyprus in March. Staging through Orange, Decimomannu, Luqa and El Adem outbound, the squadron returned as a non-stop, air-refuelled sortie, supported by Valiant tankers. This was followed by a nine aircraft deployment to Akrotiri on 13th August 1963 returning to Wattisham on 10th September.

1964 saw the application of No.111 Squadron's attractive black and yellow colour scheme to its Lightning F Mk 1A's and T Mk 4. The selection of its design was the result of a competition organised by the CO, Sqn Ldr George Black, with the winning entry being painted on a 1/72nd scale model of the Lightning made by Airfix.

On 23rd July 1964, the squadron deployed to Akrotiri, sending nine aircraft to participate in the annual Cyprus Air Defence Exercise. Interrupted by a recurrence of the internal troubles on the island, the squadron was put on an alert status to protect the Sovereign Base Area. Frequent interceptions of Greek and Turkish F-84 and F-100s were flown, although the Lightning remained unarmed, carrying only drill or acquisition Firestreak AAM rounds and even though 30mm ammunition was carried, the guns were not primed. On a lighter note, the squadron also worked up a five-ship display team whilst in Cyprus before returning to Wattisham.

During November 1964, a number of air-to-air gunnery sorties were flown, one aircraft having the seldom used four gun fit, whilst the rest used the lower gun pack only. A shortage of aircraft earlier in the year had seen the addition of two Lightning F Mk 1s to supplement the squadron's strength, then with the arrival of XP738 on 7th November, conversion to the Lightning F Mk 3 began. By early March 1965, the squadron was fully converted to its new mount. However, with the grounding of the Valiant tanker fleet in January 1965 in-flight refuelling training continued courtesy of the USAF, using KC-135 aircraft, in an exercise named 'Billy Boy'. The Boeing's rigid refuelling boom was fitted with a flexible hose and drogue, which although requiring a much different technique than that used with the hose and reel equipped Valiants, did allow this valuable training to continue until the Victor tankers came on line later in the year.

1965 also saw No.111 Squadron return to formation flying, a revival of their three years as Fighter Command's world famous team 'The Black Arrows'. Initially flying with five aircraft, the team had built up to nine by the time of the Paris Air Salon in June, where they performed a synchronised formation display with seven Gnats of 'The Red Arrows'. The last display was flown at Biggin Hill in September 1967, after which the squadron returned to its primary defence role.

In 1968 the squadron participated in a number of significant celebrations. On 4th April, the Wattisham Wing put up a formation of twenty Lightnings to salute the 50th Anniversary of the Royal Air Force. On 25th April, four of No.111 Squadron's Lightning F Mk 3s, along with representatives of all Fighter Command's squadrons, flew a flypast to mark the

Command's disbandment, and finally four aircraft took part in the flypast at the RAF Royal Review at Abingdon in June.

The squadron continued to operate from Wattisham for the next six years, its periods of operational training and QRA interspersed with the annual round of Missile Practice Camps at RAF Valley and overseas deployments to Cyprus and Malta for their Air Defence exercises.

In preparation for their disbandment, the squadron received three Lightning F Mk 6s, to give pilots who were to transfer to the Binbrook Wing, experience in handling this variant. Beginning the rundown of the Lightning force, No.111 Squadron disbanded on 30th September 1974, handing over its 'number plate' to their Phantom FGR Mk 2 equipped successors.

Below: A neat five-ship formation poses for the camera early in the squadron's Lightning days. *MoD*

111 SQUADRON

Previously flew:
Hawker Hunter F Mk 6s since November 1956.

Lightnings:
F Mk 1As from 30th March 1961.
F Mk 3s from 7th November 1964.

Bases:
Wattisham, Suffolk.

Disbanded:
30th September 1974.

Later:
Started conversion to McDonnell Douglas Phantom FGR Mk 2s in October 1974. Currently flying Panavia Tornado F Mk 3s at Leuchars, Scotland.

Badge:
In front of two swords in saltaire, a cross potent quadrat charged with three seaxes.
Motto: Adstantes - Standing by.

Well known and beloved to all 'ageing modellers' as the 'Airfix Lightning', XM192/K is seen here in its later guise as Wattisham's Gate Guard, displaying the squadron's original markings with its stylised lightning flash surrounding the nose roundel. This aircraft survives today at the Bomber County Aviation Museum, Hemswell, Lincolnshire. There is a No.23 Squadron 'zap' on the fin above No.111's Jerusalem Cross and Seaxes squadron marking. *D Hemingway*

Arriving out of the murk, this formation of No.111 Squadron Lightning F Mk 3s, put in a surprise appearance at Finningley's 1971 Battle of Britain Display. The aircraft nearest the camera is XP761/N with the other two identifiable airframes being XR711 and XP738/E.

Opposite page: Re-equipping with the Lightning F Mk 3 in late 1964, No.111 Squadron was to become Fighter Command's display team the following year. This formation shot shows off the squadron's freshly painted colourful markings based on those previously applied to their F Mk 1A's. Photographed early in 1965, these aircraft including XR715, XR714, and XR711 have not yet had their code letters applied. *MoD*

Opposite page top and this page top: Lightning F Mk 3, XP751/L, photographed at Wattisham in 1972 and later in 1974 displaying a 'Richthofen R' shield 'zap' on the nose above the lightning flash, applied during an exchange visit with the Luftwaffe unit JG 71. *D Hemingway*

Opposite page bottom: A plastic cap protects the seeker head on XP748/G's Red Top missiles. Photographed on Wattisham's flight line. *D Hemingway*

'EMPTY YOUR POCKETS', so says the stern warning to pilots, and ground crew, on the intake cover of Lightning F Mk 3, XP738/E, photographed at Wattisham. *G Kipp*

Lightning F Mk 3 XP748/G was photographed on Wattisham's flight line during the September 1972 Battle of Britain display held at No.111 Squadron's home base. This aircraft was transferred to Binbrook in October 1972 and served with No.11 Squadron until the end of 1974. After a period of open storage it was refurbished and mounted on a plinth at Binbrook's main gate in dual Nos.5 and 11 Squadron markings. *D Hemingway*

Lightning F Mk 3 XP749/K pictured at RAF Wattisham alongside all the associated ground equipment needed to get this potent jet fighter in to the air. Retained by the squadron until disbandment, this particular aircraft went on to survive with the Binbrook Wing until the final closure of the Lincolnshire Lightning base. It achieved a total of 3,212 flying hours. *D Hemingway*

Opposite page top: Lightning F Mk 3 XR713/A photographed on Wattisham's flight line prior to displaying at the 1972 Battle of Britain At Home Open Day. *D Hemingway*

Opposite page bottom: Another view of XR713/A, 'Treble One' Squadron CO's aircraft, making a late arrival for Lakenheath's 1973 Open Day, taxiing through the air show crowds to its allocated parking lot.

Acting as a spare aircraft for the display Lightning, an F Mk 3 XP696/696, of No.226 OCU, No.2T Squadron. No.111 Squadron revived their original large squadron fin badge for the final six months of Lightning operations, as seen here on XP754/R at Finningley in September 1974.

Another shot of No.111 Squadron's T Mk 5 XS421/T, displaying the final style of squadron badge marking in the summer of 1974. *G Kipp*

Opposite page top: One of a number of Lightning T Mk 5s flown by No.111 Squadron during their 'Lightning Days', XS421/T was photographed here whilst acting as a crew ferry at No.60 MU in 1972.
D Hemingway

Opposite page bottom: Having spent all of its service life with No.111 Squadron XP740/B shared its fate with most of the Wattisham Wing's F Mk 3s when it was prematurely scrapped shortly after the squadron's disbandment. Here, a once proud defender of the realm languishes on Wattisham's dump in September 1975.
D Hemingway

Returning to Leconfield in October 1962 the squadron's first aircraft in the shape of Lightning T Mk 4 XM988, the first to be delivered to a squadron had arrived, but it would be three months before their first Lightning F Mk 2 would materialise. Tasked in the intervening period with acceptance checks on this first two-seat variant, a further three 'T-Birds' arrived before the end of December and were also used in continuation training.

Although the first Lightning F Mk 2 XN775 had been delivered to Leconfield on 17th December 1962 problems with the aircraft, discovered during acceptance checks, prevented its hand-over to the squadron until the following February. However, the squadron had received its full complement of twelve Lightning F Mk 2s during March, when operational training began in earnest and there was a subsequent ending of acceptance checks on the T Mk 4.

19 SQUADRON

Whilst still flying the Hawker Hunter F Mk 6,
No.19 Squadron's pilots began their Lightning training
on the F Mk 2 simulator at Leconfield in mid-1962, before
reporting to the Lightning Conversion Squadron
at Middleton St.George.

Again, shortages of specialised equipment and trained technicians contributed to a low state of serviceability with, at one stage, the squadron being reduced to having only one working AI 23 radar set out of the twenty available. With a gradual return of serviceable aircraft and with most of the pilots having completed the day and night radar conversion courses, No.19 Squadron was declared fully operational on 1st August 1963.

The squadron's Lightnings were fitted with their in-flight refuelling probes in January 1964, in preparation for tanker training the following month. In April the squadron began its first Missile Practice Camp, at RAF Valley, the sixth by a Lightning squadron, but the most successful to date.

The squadron embarked on their first overseas deployment when the Lightnings were air refuelled en route to Akrotiri on 20th June 1964. Four days later three of these Lightnings flew on to Bahrain on a discreet mission, supported by four Valiant tankers, the purpose of which was to demonstrate the Lightning to officials of the Royal Saudi Air Force. With its squadron markings removed and flown by BAC test pilot Jimmy Dell, the aircraft XN730 gave its display to the gathered officials at Riyadh Airport on 4th July, which undoubtedly helped secure the largest British military export order to date.

In 1965, the squadron began their first tanker trials with the Victor K Mk 1, which had begun to replace the hastily withdrawn Valiants that had been grounded by serious airframe fatigue problems. The squadron's first Victor supported exercise took place in July 1965 during the return of four Lightnings from a Cyprus deployment.

From the end of spring 1965, most of No.19 Squadron's aircraft were configured with four 30mm ADEN cannon, the lower pair replacing the Firestreak air-to-air missile pack, prior to its announced move to 2nd Allied Tactical Air Force, West Germany, later in the year. Gun firing and limited ground attack training was practiced over the North Sea ranges. Prior to their departure, the squadron fulfilled its requirement to supply aircraft for static display at Waddington's and Finningley's 'Battle of Britain at Home' days, also providing a four ship display team at both venues.

The move to Gütersloh, along with their twin-seat Hunter T Mk 7, took place on 23rd September and after a quick turnaround, No.19 Squadron launched their four ship team to mark their arrival. The squadron was declared fully operational on 6th October 1965 and they quickly settled into the routine of exercises, exchange visits and QRA's, interspersed with continental air show appearances, generally with its four ship team.

In 1968, the Lightning F Mk 2 airframes started to be returned to Warton for modification to nearer the standard of the long-range Lightning F Mk 6 variant. The modifications included a cambered wing leading edge, square top fin, ventral fuel pack and airfield arrester hook due to the F Mk 2s higher weight. Incorporating most of the ultimate Lightning's features, including the cambered wing leading edge, larger fin and large integral ventral fuel tank. Uniquely, the nose cannon were retained on the Lightning F Mk 2A, as the variant was to be known. However, unlike the F Mk 6, the new wings were not stressed to carry overwing tanks and the aircraft remained capable of only operating the Firestreak air-to-air missile.

With virtually no spare aircraft within either Nos.19 or 92 Squadrons, the modification process was slow as each squadron was only able to release one or two aircraft at a time to the programme. Despatching their first aircraft XN730 out on 4th October 1966, the first 'new' F Mk 2A XN789 was received back by the squadron on 15th January 1968. No.19 Squadron was not back to full strength until February 1970, when a complement of twelve F Mk 2A's, two F Mk 2s for TFF duties and a T Mk 4 were recorded.

Unlike the other early Lightning squadrons, No.19 never applied any colourful markings to their aircraft, displaying only their blue and white checks flanking the nose roundel in an asymmetric pattern fore and aft and its 'dolphin' squadron badge on the fin. On receiving their Lightning F Mk 2A's, the nose checks were amended into a symmetrical pattern, three rows forward and three rearward. With the aircraft increasingly operating in a low level role, they began to receive NATO

Below: XN781/B and XN776/C depart Gütersloh on a June 1971 training sortie. G Kipp

Dark Green camouflage to their upper surfaces from the spring of 1972, with a consequent reduction on the size of their squadron markings.

Despite the Lightning F Mk 2A's having recently undergone major overhauls and a complete electrical re-wiring at No.60 MU Leconfield, the low-level role was beginning to take its toll on the airframes' fatigue lives. With Phantom FGR Mk 2s now being released for the Air Defence role by their previous operators, No.19 Squadron disbanded as a Lightning unit on 31st December 1976, passing on a number of their aircraft with lower airframe hours to No.92 Squadron.

19 SQUADRON

Previously flew:
Hawker Hunter F Mk 6s since October 1956.

Lightnings:
F Mk 2s from 17th December 1962.
F Mk 2As from 15th January 1968.

Bases:
Leconfield, Yorkshire.
Gütersloh, West Germany, from 23rd September 1965.

Disbanded:
31st December 1976.

Later:
Started conversion to McDonnell Douglas Phantom FGR Mk 2s in July 1976.
Currently flying BAe Hawk T Mk 1s and T Mk 1As as part of 4 Flying Training School, RAF Valley, Wales.

Badge:
A dolphin descending between wings elevated.
Motto: Possunt quia posse videntur -
They can because they think they can.

Opposite page top: Retained in its F Mk 2 configuration after the rest of the squadron had re-equipped with converted F Mk 2A's XN794/W was one of two Lightnings used by the unit in the Target Facilities role. *G Kipp*

Opposite page bottom: F Mk 2 XN779/X at Gütersloh in July 1971. The ports for the 30mm ADEN cannon are visible in the upper nose. *G Kipp*

Lightning F Mk 2, XN787/M at No.60 MU Leconfield in July 1968, undergoing a Fire Integrity Modification programme. Initially No.19 Squadron applied their blue and white chequers in an 'asymmetric pattern' on the nose, five forward and three aft of the roundel.

The F Mk 2A conversion embodied some of the features of the Mk 6, but retained the 30mm ADEN nose cannon armament and only Firestreak missiles could be carried. Photographed in 1971, the nose markings were now symmetrical as seen in this shot of XN724/F, in one of Gütersloh's blast pens. *G Kipp*

Lightning F Mk 2A's XN731/Z and XN789/J, (the latter being the first F Mk 2A received by the squadron in January 1968), on approach to Gütersloh. Lacking its nose markings, XN789 had just returned to the unit after an overhaul at No.60 MU when this photograph was taken in March 1972. *G Kipp*

Lightning F Mk 2A XN735/A photographed lining up on Gütersloh's runway in June 1972. It has an application of protective lacquer on the undercarriage, this being a common feature on many of Gütersloh's Lightnings. *G Kipp*

Opposite page top: Lightning F Mk 2A XN771/P recently returned from Warton after receiving Fire Integrity Modifications, about to land at Gütersloh in the summer of 1971. *G Kipp*

Opposite page bottom: Braking parachutes are an essential part of any Lightning landing, as demonstrated, in perfect harmony, by Lightning F Mk 2A's XN781/B and XN776/C of No.19 Squadron in July 1971. *G Kipp*

Line-up of No.19 Squadron's Lightnings on Gütersloh's apron in 1972. As well as being the first F Mk 2A delivered to No.19 Squadron, XN789/J in the foreground, was also the first F Mk 2A to undergo the major servicing programme at No.60 MU. Lightning T Mk 4, XM991/T can be seen immediately behind XN789. *G Kipp*

Its shiny natural metal days nearly over, Lightning F Mk 2A XN790/L returns to Gütersloh in the late autumn sunshine of October 1972. *G Kipp*

Opposite page top: Prior to having their NATO Dark Green camouflage applied, Gütersloh's Lightnings had the red, white and blue national markings on the upper surfaces of the wings, fuselage and fin sides toned down to the 'tactical' red/blue style, as seen here on F Mk 2A XN781/B in the autumn of 1972. Note the areas where the original markings have been scrubbed off and the reduced size of the nose roundel and squadron markings. *G Kipp*

Opposite page bottom: One of No.19 Squadron's 'T-Birds', Lightning T Mk 4 XM973/V on approach into a stormy Gütersloh, circa September 1972. Already prepared to received its NATO Dark Green upper surface camouflage scheme, the areas where the original markings have been scrubbed off are readily apparent around the reduced size nose roundel and squadron markings on the fin. *G Kipp*

Above: Beginning in 1972, Gütersloh's Lightnings began to receive NATO Dark Green camouflage to their upper surfaces. Lightning F Mk 2A's XN724/F and XN771/P illustrate the new toned-down look in the summer of 1974. The under surfaces and intake nose ring remained in the original natural metal finish. *G Kipp*

Opposite page top: Long serving Lightning T Mk 4 XM991/T was flown by No.19 Squadron from September 1963 to October 1975, at which time it was struck off charge. Seen here in its glorious silver days in the early spring of 1971. *G Kipp*

Opposite page bottom: Lightning F Mk 2A XN776/C on 'finals' at Gütersloh in the autumn of 1975. XN776 served exclusively with No.19 Squadron until the squadron stood down on 31st December 1976 to re-equip with Phantom FGR Mk 2s. This aircraft then served briefly with No.92 Squadron until they too stood down. In May 1982, it was acquired by the Museum of Flight, East Fortune, where it is now on display. *G Kipp*

92 SQUADRON

As the second squadron in the Leconfield Wing, No.92's conversion followed the pattern set by No.19 Squadron, with pilots beginning their conversion to the type with the Lightning Conversion Squadron at Middleton St.George.

On their return to Leconfield, training on the Lightning T Mk 4s continued until the arrival of their first Lightning F Mk 2 XN783 on 26th March 1963. Enough aircraft had arrived by April for conversion training to begin in earnest, with the full unit establishment being completed by June.

Unlike their sister squadron No.92 preferred a more colourful approach to flying the Lightning and promptly painted the fins of their aircraft in a Royal Blue as a reminder of their previous status as the 'Blue Diamonds' aerobatic team flying the Hunter F Mk 6.

Although operational training was hindered by the usual serviceability problems, with both the aircraft and its AI 23 radar, conversion training was disrupted in August for the squadron to practice for its participation in the forthcoming 'Battle of Britain at Home Day' celebrations, for which it supplied a five aircraft formation team. The squadron was declared operational on 1st October 1963, and stood their first period of QRA in November.

1964 began with a Missile Practice Camp at RAF Valley, the first for a Lightning squadron, with six aircraft including the T Mk 4 attending in January. A start was made on in-flight refuelling training in April but by May the Lightnings serviceability rate reached an all time low with many of the defects requiring lengthy periods 'on the hangar floor'. In September 1964 No.92 Squadron were tasked to provide six aircraft to represent Fighter Command at the SBAC Show at Farnborough, with displays at Biggin Hill and Finningley the following week. The squadron was then returned to their operation commitments.

The year ended with further in-flight refuelling training in readiness for a deployment to Cyprus planned for the New Year. In the event, the four aircraft involved staged through Geilenkirchen, Istres, Decimomannu, Luqa and El Adem due to problems with the Valiant tanker fleet, finally arriving at Akrotiri on 8th January. With the Valiant fleet now permanently grounded, this turned out to be a rather protracted deployment as the aircraft did not return to Leconfield until 3rd June 1965 when No.19 Squadron relieved them.

As with its sister squadron, No.92 Squadron aircraft were configured with four 30mm ADEN cannon to enable some air-to-ground gunnery practice prior to its planned move to RAF Germany. This secondary ground attack capability was considered to be desirable in its new environment. The move to Geilenkirchen was completed over the two days 29th to 30th December with the squadron returned to operational status by 7th January 1966. The more crowded skies over Northern Europe provided the squadron and intercept controllers excellent training value with targets ranging from T-33s to supersonic F-104 Starfighters now established in widespread service in the NATO air forces.

After just two years in their new home, No.92 Squadron moved again, this time to rejoin No.19 Squadron at Gütersloh in January 1968. It was deemed more economical and practical to operate both the German-based Lightning squadrons from the same station. They also shared their Battle Flight commitments, each maintaining a pair of Lightnings all year around, on alternating months. Because of its close proximity to the former East German border, scrambles by the Gütersloh Alert Force were relatively frequent – but not always to warn off possible Eastern Bloc incursions in NATO airspace. On occasions, civil aircraft, often lacking any sophisticated navigational equipment required the presence of Lightnings to remind them of their proximity to the Iron Curtain.

Re-equipment with the Lightning F Mk 2A began on 26th June 1968 with the delivery of XN773 from Warton and, as with No.19 Squadron, the build up was to be a slow process spread over two years. Two of the squadron's Lightning F Mk 2s, XN768 and XN769 remained unconverted and were used as 'target' aircraft for practice interceptions until their withdrawal in mid 1973.

Although the aircrafts' blue fin and spine survived until 1970, several years after the toning down of the rest of the RAF's Lightning fleet, the red and yellow arrowhead marking had been revised sometime earlier to a more conformist, checked, design in the squadron's colours. The CO's aircraft XN793 was the last aircraft to retain its colourful markings and natural metal finish, reprieved by a spell in the MU, but then it finally succumbed to the NATO Dark Green camouflaged upper surfaces in 1972.

Both of Gütersloh's squadrons enjoyed an active round of exchange visits with other NATO units, interspersed with the annual Missile Practice Camp at Valley and deployments to Decimomannu for gun firing, taking full advantage of the favourable Mediterranean climate.

Below: High above Germany this 92 Squadron pair break formation for the camera ship. Circa 1972. *NWHG*

With the Sepecat Jaguar rapidly filling the RAF's tactical roles of ground attack and reconnaissance, No.92 Squadron followed their sister squadron's conversion to the Phantom FGR Mk 2, finally disbanding as a Lightning operator on 31st March 1977.

92 SQUADRON

Previously flew:
Hawker Hunter F Mk 6s since February 1957.

Lightnings:
F Mk 2s from 26th March 1963.
F Mk 2As from 26th June 1968.

Bases:
Leconfield, Yorkshire.
Geilenkirchen, West Germany, from 29th December 1965.
Gütersloh, West Germany, from 22nd January 1968.

Later:
Started conversion to McDonnell-Douglas Phantom FGR Mk 2s in January 1977. Finally disbanded as part of No.7 Flying Training School at Chivenor, Devon, flying BAe Hawk T Mk 1As on 1st October 1994.

Badge:
A cobra entwining a sprig of maple.
Name: 'East India'.
Motto: Aut pugna aut morere - Either fight or die.

Above: Relinquishing their role as the 'Blue Diamonds' aerobatic team equipped with Hunter F Mk 6s, No 92 Squadron transitioned to the Lightning F Mk 2 at Leconfield in early 1963. XN733/L was photographed there circa 1965. Almost immediately on receiving the new aircraft, the blue fin and red and yellow nose arrowhead markings were applied, the former to maintain their 'Blue Diamond' link. *R Lindsay*

Opposite page top: The blue fin was extended to include the spine from mid-1964 and a white outline was applied around the nose roundel and arrowhead marking in time for their appearance at the SBAC Farnborough Show in September, having been re-appointed as Fighter Command's aerobatic team for that year. Lightning F Mk 2 XN732/H captured here taking off from Gütersloh, displays the new scheme perfectly. *G Kipp*

Opposite page bottom: Lightning T Mk 4 XM995/T was received in November 1962 and remained on strength with No.92 Squadron until the unit disbanded on 31st March 1977. Photographed here after both squadrons of the Leconfield Wing had relocated to RAF Germany, XM995/T is resplendent in No.92's colourful squadron markings and blue trim. *G Kipp*

Above: Apparently forming the centre piece of a No.92 Squadron 'occasion', the suitably marked-up Battle of Britain Flight Spitfire Mk Vb AB910, (coded QJ as per the unit's World War II codes), was photographed at Leconfield, c1964 to1965. Sharing the ASP with the blue-finned No.92 Squadron F Mk 2s, are F Mk 2s of No.19 Squadron. *NWHG Warton*

Opposite page top: As with No.19 Squadron, No.92 Squadron retained a pair of F Mk 2s for target duties. XN768/S photographed at Gütersloh in March 1971, also managed to retain its blue fin and spine until eventually being camouflaged. From 1968 the squadron's more familiar red and yellow checks replaced the 'arrowhead' nose markings. *G Kipp*

Opposite page bottom: Parked on one of Gütersloh's dispersals in April 1972, Lightning F Mk 2A XN727/W sports the standardised 'bar' of red and yellow check form of No.92 Squadron's markings. Although the lower 30mm ADEN cannon ports are visible on this aircraft, they were not carried as evidenced by the Firestreak AAM pack being in place. *G Kipp*

Opposite page top: XN793/A was the last No.92 Squadron Lightning F Mk 2A to retain its blue fin and spine before being finally camouflaged. Photographed at Gütersloh in May 1971, it could surely only be a coincidence that it was the CO's aircraft at the time. *G Kipp*

Opposite page bottom: A relatively rare photograph of a four-gun Lightning F Mk 2A, the missile pack being replaced by

two 30mm ADEN cannon positioned under the nose. This photograph of XN792/M was taken on approach to Gütersloh in May 1971. *G Kipp*

Top: XM968/Q in the foreground, was the second Lightning T Mk 4 on strength with No.92 Squadron, from early 1972 until it had the dubious distinction of being the Gütersloh Wing's last loss when it crashed near the airfield on 24th

February 1977. Both crew members escaped. Behind are Lightning F Mk 2As XN782/H and XN775/B. *G Kipp*

Above: All three of No.92 Squadron's Lightning variants and Lightning colour schemes are seen in this shot taken circa 1973. Headed by F Mk 2A XN730/J which was the squadron's first camouflaged aircraft, the T Mk 4 is XM968/Q and the F Mk 2 still with a blue fin is XN768/S. *G Kipp*

Top: Stripped of most of its original colours and ready for the NATO Dark Green upper surface paint finish, Lightning T Mk 4 XM968/Q was photographed at Gütersloh in the summer of 1972. It features incomplete nose markings still awaiting the yellow checks and it has a section of the spine finished in a dark colour. *G Kipp*

Above: A beautiful blue sky adds a touch of colour to the sombre NATO Dark Green camouflaged F Mk 2A XN773/E, photographed at Gütersloh in the summer of 1975. *G Kipp*

Opposite page top: The white Firestreak air-to-air missiles contrast sharply against the otherwise drab appearance of the NATO Dark Green camouflaged No.92 Squadron F Mk 2A, XN774/F at Gütersloh in the summer of 1975. *G Kipp*

Opposite page bottom: An evocative photograph of a 'pairs landing' by Lightning F Mk 2A's, XN787/L and XN782/H at Gütersloh in the summer of 1976. With the fatigue life of the aircraft nearing expiry, No.92 Squadron began re-equipping with Phantom FGR Mk 2s and stood down as a Lightning squadron on 31st March 1977. *G Kipp*

23 SQUADRON

After a somewhat nomadic association with the Javelin, flying from such far flung and exotic locations as Karachi and Tengah amongst their many deployments, No.23 Squadron moved into a more settled lifestyle at Leuchars in March 1963.

Ceasing to be an operational Javelin squadron on 1st October 1964, they re-formed with the Lightning on the same day.

Their first two brand new F Mk 3s XP707 and XP708 had already arrived earlier on 18th August, and the squadron crews were mostly experienced Lightning pilots posted from other units. The other pilots, though eager to begin conversion to the type, had to settle for training on the F Mk 3 flight simulator until the end of the month, as the aircraft were still undergoing acceptance checks and ground crew familiarisation training. The CO Sqn Ldr John McLeod in XP756 made the squadron's inaugural flight on 29th September on a photographic formation sortie with one of the soon to be withdrawn Javelins.

A fairly rapid build up of aircraft saw the full complement of twelve F Mk 3s and a T Mk 4, received by the end of October. They were all painted with a white fin and spine to rival co-located No.74 Squadron with their black finned machines. With training well advanced, No.23 Squadron was declared operational at the end of December.

Operating alongside No.74 Squadron at this most northerly fighter base, with their F Mk 3s, they became the RAF's premier fighter wing with an almost daily trade in Soviet long-range reconnaissance aircraft to be investigated, flying down through the Faroes/Shetland Gap. Highlighting the F Mk 3s woefully short endurance and compounded by the Valiant tankers premature retirement, the squadron soon began in-flight refuelling training with exercise 'Billy Boy' and the USAF's KC-135 tankers in April 1965. The Boeing tankers were also engaged during operational QRA interceptions until the Victor tankers became available later in the year.

No.23 Squadron stood their first period of QRA in February 1966 and an increasing involvement in a number of exercises added stimulus to the operational training task. The squadron detached six aircraft to RAF Valley for their first Missile Practice Camp in August and at the same time began in-flight refuelling training with the new Victor tankers, with eight sorties flown by the end of the month. For the forthcoming Battle of Britain at Home Day celebrations in September the squadron provided a four ship team called 'Eagle Red' for Leuchar's air show.

On October 27th, four F Mk 3s departed on the squadron's first deployment to Cyprus. Whilst there, one of their aircraft XP735 accompanied by XS450 of No.111 Squadron flew to Jordan where they were tasked with displaying the Lightning to King Hussein and the Royal Jordanian Air Force. They arrived at Amman on 6th December and returned to Akrotiri on the 9th.

With No.74 Squadron due to depart to the Far East in June 1967, No.11 Squadron began to reform at Leuchars with the F Mk 6 on 1st April, creating a three Lightning squadron wing, albeit briefly. With the delivery of Interim F Mk 6 XR761 from No.60 MU on 8th May, No.23 Squadron began the transition to the ultimate long-range variant of this fighter. By August they had received their first four full production standard models including XS938, the last F Mk 6 built. The year closed with a detachment of four aircraft to the Royal Norwegian Air Force base at Sola on 26th October, and six Lightnings detached to RAF Valley to participate in a joint RAF/RN exercise in November.

Now fully equipped with the full standard F Mk 6, six aircraft were detached to Wattisham on 4th June 1968 to take part in the Royal Review flypasts while the remainder of No.23 Squadron with their five F Mk 6s and T Mk 5 held QRA at Leuchars. They were to witness a record period of alert activity with fifteen operational scrambles called during the period 4th to 7th July, resulting in ten successful interceptions of Soviet long-range reconnaissance aircraft. As a testament to the improving maintenance situation a 100% serviceability rate was achieved for this period.

In an interesting aside to more normal overseas deployments, two of the squadron's Lightnings made their first Atlantic crossing on exercise 'Maple Ranger' when XR725/A and XS936/B flew non-stop to Toronto to participate in the Canadian International Air Show. Initially departing Leuchars on 26th August, the aircraft were forced to return when XS936 developed a fuel leak in one of its overwing tanks. However they completed the journey the following day and accompanied by the Victor tankers, the flight was accomplished in 7 hours 20 minutes. The squadron was also declared operational with the Red Top missile in August, firing their first five rounds during a December Missile Practice Camp at RAF Valley.

Between 21st and 28th September 1970, No.23 Squadron paid a goodwill visit to Sweden where they were the first RAF fighters to visit the country for more than ten years. Taking with them four of their F Mk 6s and the T Mk 5, this visit had been preceded a few weeks beforehand by a visit from a Soviet Air Force MiG-21 squadron, an interesting comparison of types for the Swedish hosts. This month also saw a reduction of all Lightning squadrons complement of aircraft from twelve to ten plus a trainer, and a corresponding reduction in the number of pilots from fifteen to thirteen.

After the long lamented loss of the aircraft's built-in gun armament from the F Mk 3 and F Mk 6 variants, a number of No.23 Squadron aircraft had a trial installation of two 30mm ADEN cannon fitted in the forward section of the ventral fuel tank during early 1971. With the first test firing on 26th March and subsequent test proving satisfactory, this became a standard fit with all the F Mk 6 squadrons.

With the departure of No.11 Squadron to Binbrook in March 1972, No.23 Squadron then became the sole Lightning unit at Leuchars sharing its base with No.43 Squadron and their Phantom FG Mk 1s, whose longer range and greater weapons capacity were more able to fulfil the northern QRA tasks. No.23 Squadron remained active until 31st October 1975 when its 'number plate' was taken over by a newly-formed Phantom squadron.

Below: XR761, displaying 23 Squadron's early fin badge, prepares to depart on a sortie from Leuchars in September 1971. *R Lindsay*

23 SQUADRON

Previously flew:
Gloster Javelin FAW Mk 9s from April 1960.

Lightnings:
F Mk 3s from 1st October 1964
F Mk 6s from 8th May 1967.

Bases:
Leuchars, Scotland, throughout.

Disbanded:
31st October 1975.

Later:
McDonnell-Douglas Phantom FGR Mk 2s from December 1975; Panavia Tornado F Mk 3s from November 1988. Currently flying as part of the Waddington AEW Wing with Boeing Sentry AEW Mk 1s.

Badge:
An eagle preying on a falcon.
Motto: Semper aggressus - Always having attacked.

XP707/A was one of the first two Lightning F Mk 3s delivered to newly re-formed No.23 Squadron at Leuchars on 18th August 1964. This was the first single-seat fighter the squadron had operated after a period of thirty-one years flying multi-crewed types. The fin and spine of the aircraft were soon painted white to rival the co-located No.74 Squadron's black-finned F Mk 3s.

Being the most northerly of the RAF's UK airfields, Leuchars gave plenty of opportunity for its based Lightnings to intercept Soviet aircraft nearing British airspace, highlighting the woefully short endurance of the F Mk 3. Receiving Interim Lightning Mk 6s in May 1967 somewhat eased the problem of range, although interception sorties still required tanker assistance. This Lightning F Mk 6 XR753/A was photographed escorting a Russian Tu-95 'Bear' in 1972. *NWHG Warton*

By early 1968, No.23 Squadron was fully equipped with full production standard Lightning F Mk 6s. XR753/A was put on display at Leconfield, whilst resident with No.60 MU to receive Fire Integrity Modifications in July 1974. Seen with its FOD guard in place, ground engine runs were soon to begin before its return to the squadron.

During its last year of Lightning operations, the CO's aircraft was painted with the white fin and spine as worn on its early F Mk 3s. XR753/A was photographed on Valley's flight line in August 1975. This aircraft ended its service with No.11 Squadron at Binbrook and is still preserved by the squadron at their current home at RAF Leeming.
M C Bursell

Wheeling to starboard high above the clouds, 23 Squadron's four-ship team 'Eagle Red' appeared at a number of air shows shortly after re-equipping with F Mk 6s. This formation comprises XR728, 747, 754 and XS937. c1970. *NWHG Warton*

Taxiing out at Leconfield for a post overhaul test flight, Lightning F Mk 6 XR754/M gleams in the sunlight of spring 1971. On its return to the squadron, based at Leuchars, it was re-coded 'D'.
D Hemingway

Opposite page top: Lightning F Mk 6 XR760/H was photographed on arrival at 60 MU Leconfield for a major service in September 1970. It would still be a year before its missile armament was augmented by the belly tank mounted cannons.
D Hemingway

Opposite page bottom: Seen on the opposite page as 'M', XR754 was later re-coded 'D' and was photographed here on finals at Leuchars in the summer of 1973 with its full weapons fit.
G Kipp

Opposite page top: Lightning F Mk 6, XS935/J returns to its Hard Standing at Leuchars after a sortie over the North Sea. *G Kipp*

Opposite page bottom: No.23 Squadron received three Lightning F Mk 3s for both target training and operational use during May 1974, comprising XP706/R, XP750/P and photographed here XP751/Q, on approach to Leuchars in June 1974. *G Kipp*

Photographed at Leuchars in June 1973, XS927/O appears to have suffered an attack by the Airfix riveter on its nose. The Red Top drill round lacks its forward fins, a common practice with all F Mk 6 Squadrons, effectively reducing stress loads on both the missile body and the airframe. *G Kipp*

At the end of a short loan to No.23 Squadron, Lightning T Mk 4, XS421/S arrived at No.60 MU Leconfield in April 1975, where its empty hulk is seen here receiving attention. Its last flight was to Binbrook at the end of June where the aircraft was placed in open storage.

Gaining experience with a Hunter T Mk 7A specially modified with the OR946 instrumentation of the Lightning F Mk 3 and F Mk 6, it was not until 19th November that their first Lightning T Mk 5 XS451 was delivered to Binbrook.

The first Interim F Mk 6s arrived at Binbrook on 10th December and the squadron began a slow build up of its training programme with progress being hampered by bad weather in January and February. As the squadron had formed with a cadre of experienced Lightning pilots, emphasis was given to pilots new to the aircraft. With the delivery of its last two Lightnings in March, flying hours and the tempo of the training increased. The squadron were even able to fly its first five-ship formation for the benefit of the ground crews at Binbrook.

5 SQUADRON

Disbanding as a Javelin squadron at Geilenkirchen on the 7th October 1965, No.5 Squadron reformed at Binbrook the following day, thus gaining the distinction of becoming the first operator of the Lightning F Mk 6, albeit the Interim variant.

In April, five of the squadron's F Mk 6s along with their T Mk 5 detached to RAF Valley for their first Missile Practice Camp, where although only two Firestreak rounds were fired, both were successful. The remainder of the squadron at Binbrook became involved in exercise 'Co-op', called on 20th April during which their depleted numbers were ably assisted by the Lightnings and pilots of the Fighter Command Trials Unit, co-located at Binbrook. This month also saw the commencement of in-flight refuelling training with the Victors.

The squadron stood its first period of southern QRA on 20th May, taking over from Wattisham and also began the first of many overseas deployments on 26th June, with four aircraft to Cyprus supported by Victor tankers. On a longer route proving exercise, four aircraft departed for the Persian Gulf base at Masirah on 1st November, staging through Akrotiri. Back at Binbrook, the squadron rehearsed a five-ship formation to celebrate their 50th year of continuous service on 25th November.

With the arrival of XS922 on 30th December, re-equipping with the full production standard F Mk 6 began and the full complement was received by the end of March 1967. With ten of these aircraft, No.5 Squadron deployed to Luqa on 6th October in support of exercise 'Forthright 67', the annual Malta Air Defence Exercise. Returning to Binbrook at the end of the month, all of the squadrons' aircraft had been decorated with a day-glo Maltese Cross on their fins as a mark of respect to their hosts, a tradition which was to last for a number of years.

After its return to Binbrook, normal operational training was hampered by the weather during November and in order to attain the required flying hours for the month, over fifty sorties were flown in one day.

The squadron lost its first aircraft in January 1968 while on a detachment to Leuchars to undertake a period of northern QRA. Shortly after take off XS900 suffered a control restriction and was abandonded off the coast with the pilot successfully ejecting. Continuing a bad start to the year, XS924 was lost in a flying accident, crashing near Binbrook on 29th April, with the pilot tragically losing his life.

Following a period of good serviceability No.5 Squadron also lost four aircraft to the hangar floor in April. With the aircraft now approaching 500 flying hours, fuel leaks, which dogged the Lightning throughout its service life began to be a major concern, especially as they were not confined to any particular components but manifested themselves at random.

On a more positive note, events during 1969 included a four-ship formation flypast over Buckingham Palace in June to mark the Queen's birthday and the participation in an eighteen Lightning formation over Caernarfon on 1st July for the Investiture of the Prince of Wales.

In a repeat of a similar event flown the previous year by No.23 Squadron, two of the squadron's aircraft XS902 and XS922 flew to Andrews Air Force Base on exercise 'Canus Ranger' on 12th August, as a goodwill visit to the USA and Canada. The aircraft were displayed at three major air shows during their tour which ended at the Toronto International Air Show, and they returned home on 4th September.

The end of the year saw the squadron heavily engaged in in-flight refuelling training with Victor tankers to get the pilots qualified for the forthcoming exercise 'Ultimacy', a deployment of ten of their Lightnings to Singapore. Departing in pairs or threes during 8th to 11th December, the aircraft broke the journey with a stop-over at Masirah. The major event of the deployment was a joint air defence exercise held with No.74 Squadron, other locally based RAF squadrons and RAAF Mirages, demonstrating between them Strike Commands ability to re-enforce their Far Eastern bases. Before their return to Binbrook in January 1970, No.5 Squadron exchanged four of their aircraft with four from No.74 Squadron that required major servicing and delivered them to No.60 MU for attention.

During 13th to 16th April a team of six pilots and aircraft competing in the annual AFCENT competition won outright and were presented with the Huddleston Trophy. The feat was repeated the following year, which resulted in the permanent retention of the trophy by the squadron. 1970 also saw them win them the Dacre Trophy that was awarded for the best overall performance by a UK fighter squadron.

Although No.5 Squadron has been responsible for maintaining the Binbrook Target Facilities Flight's F Mk 1 and F Mk 1A's, these aircraft were absorbed by the squadron in June 1970 and were marked in the squadron's colours that now included the addition of a large red number '5' encircling the fin badge. The F Mk 1A's were handed back to the reformed TFF in September 1972 and the squadron was augmented with two F Mk 3s, although from 1973 three were normally on charge. In addition to their target role, the F Mk 3s were also used operationally with an additional role of display flying at air shows, thus preserving the fatigue life of the F Mk 6s.

Having been joined by No.11 Squadron in March 1972, both squadrons of the Binbrook Wing temporally relocated to RAF Leconfield in Yorkshire for two six month periods in 1973 and 1976, allowing runway repairs to be carried out at their home base.

With the disbandment of No.23 Squadron in October 1975, Binbrook was to be the last bastion of Lightning operations in the UK. From this time onwards, always under the threat of disbandment, Nos.5 and 11 Squadrons continued in their Air Defence role for many more years. Highlights of this period included Binbrook's 25th Lightning Anniversary celebrations on 3rd August 1979. Here a line-up of aircraft was painted in all their previous squadrons' colours, although sadly on camouflaged airframes. An intended twenty-five Lightning formation flypast was unfortunately cancelled due to inclement weather on the day. To celebrate its own 21st Anniversary of Lightning operations, No.5 Squadron's reunion was held in beautiful late autumn sunshine on 7th November 1986. This event produced a diamond nine formation which 'beat up' the airfield before landing.

With a gradual run down in operations towards the end of 1987, No.5 Squadron disbanded in late December, handing over to a Tornado F Mk 3 squadron and ended a twenty-two year association of operating the same aircraft type from the same airfield.

5 SQUADRON

Previously flew:
Gloster Javelin FAW Mk 9s from November 1962.

Lightnings:
F Mk 6s from 30th December 1965.

Bases:
Binbrook, Lincolnshire, throughout.

Disbanded:
31st December 1987.

Later:
Panavia Tornado F Mk 3s from December 1987, disbanding 2003. Currently working up (as a ground party) at Waddington, Lincolnshire, to operate the Raytheon Sentinel R Mk 1 ASTOR.

Badge:
A maple leaf. Motto: Frangas non flectas – Thou mayst break but shall not bend me.

Below: To celebrate the second successive year of winning the coveted AFCENT competition the squadron was awarded the Huddleston Trophy, 5 Squadron put up this eleven-ship formation in April 1971.

No.3 Crash Gate at RAF Binbrook was an aviation enthusiast's heaven, once security at this Lincolnshire airfield was relaxed around 1970. It is surprising to reflect that in that era of lovely 'silver' Lightnings, such as illustrated by this F Mk 6 XS895/B photographed in August 1972, and its squadron mates, were witnessed by no more than a handful of enthusiasts until the advent of camouflage in the mid-1970s.

Returning from its final sortie of the day, Lightning F Mk 6 XR726/N complete with overwing tanks, soaks up the last rays of the evening sunshine at Leconfield in September 1973. Runway repairs at Binbrook in both 1973 and 1976 were the cause of these temporary re-locations north, to this even more photograph-friendly location.

Opposite page top: Lightning T Mk 4 XS455/T at Binbrook in July 1972, had a short, but incident packed service career, which culminated in its loss into the North Sea in September 1972, following a hydraulic failure. Both crew members ejected successfully.

Opposite page bottom: The Binbrook Wing's 1973 Leconfield deployment began on 1st May, with most of No.5 Squadron's aircraft arriving fitted with overwing fuel tanks, which they retained for most of their stay until returning home in late September. F Mk 6 XS898/K seen here, is about to turn onto the runway for another sortie.

Opposite page top: RAF Binbrook was the first Lightning Wing station to benefit from the introduction of supersonic targets in the shape of early F Mk 1 and F Mk 1A Lightning models adapted specifically for this role. Originally formed as an autonomous unit in June 1967 as the Binbrook Target Facilities Flight their two aircraft were briefly taken on charge by No.5 Squadron between 1971 and 72. F Mk 1A XM183/X seen here, was photographed in April 1972.

Opposite page bottom: Lightning F Mk 6s XR723/D and XR752/H 'put on the power' for a thunderous 'pairs take-off' from Leconfield in the summer of 1976. Nos.5 and 11 Squadrons were again deployed to this temporary Yorkshire base whilst runway repairs were being carried out at Binbrook.

Above: With the first puff of tyre smoke just visible, Lightning F Mk 6 XR726/N impacts Leconfield's runway in June 1976. Retained by the Binbrook Wing for its entire service life, this aircraft went on to achieve an impressive 3,976.25 flying hours.

Above: A light north easterly breeze made ideal conditions for this June 1976 pairs landing by F Mk 6s XS925/L and XR752/H at Leconfield. XS925 is now on display at the RAF Museum, Hendon, in the markings of No.11 Squadron.

Opposite page top: The penultimate Lightning T Mk 5 built XV328/T makes a smoky return to Leconfield in July 1976. Taken on charge by No.5 Squadron in January 1973, this Lightning had the distinction of being the only brand new aircraft delivered to No.29 Squadron when they re-equipped with F Mk 3s in May 1967.

Opposite page bottom: Lining up for a pairs take-off in August 1976, Lightning F Mk 3s XR718/S and XP753/O display both the old natural metal and rapidly encroaching new camouflage schemes. Only recently received by No.5 Squadron, the Canadian Maple Leaf on the tail marking on XR718 is still incomplete. The aircraft's highly polished natural metal finish would soon be replaced by Dark Green and Dark Sea Grey camouflage on the upper surfaces.

Opposite page top: The last of Binbrook's Lightnings had been camouflaged in the Dark Green and Dark Sea Grey upper surface pattern by the end of October 1977. Black code letters began to be replaced by more visible white ones some two years later, as seen here on F Mk 6 XS922/C.

Opposite page bottom: A two letter code system was introduced on to the Binbrook Wing's Lightnings in the early 1980s. No.5 Squadron was allocated the prefix letter A as seen on this F Mk 3 XR716/AQ photographed in April 1987.

Undergoing replenishment between sorties at Binbrook, Lightning T Mk 5 XS416/AT has its LOX system topped up in July 1982. An undercarriage collapse on this aircraft on 19th July 1984 resulted in a restriction being placed on all of the surviving Lightning T Mk 5s to be flown with the undercarriage locked in the 'down' position until remedial modifications were carried out.

To celebrate No.5 Squadron's 21st anniversary of operating the Lightning in October 1987, a number of their aircraft received special markings. The CO's aircraft F Mk 6 XR770/AA received an all red painted fin, which was later extended to the aircraft's spine and wing leading edges.

Opposite page: Beginning in early 1982, various 'grey' camouflage schemes started to be applied to many of Binbrook's Lightnings, the result of trials with low-visibility green and grey shades having originally begun in 1978, although it did not completely replace the Dark Green and Dark Sea Grey pattern camouflage. F Mk 6s XR724/AE

nearest the camera, and XR763/AP conveniently display two of the four variations of 'grey schemes' used.

Top: Lightning F Mk 6 XS932/AG one of No.5 Squadron's 21st anniversary nine-ship formation, is seen here landing back at

RAF Binbrook in October 1987. Note the reduced size and modified, squadron markings and red bars on the fin.

Above: Making a fast low-level pass on its return to Binbrook in October 1987 F Mk 6 XS933/AJ displays another variation of the overall grey scheme.

Having previously operated the Javelin at Geilenkirchen in Germany, this was to become the first time in 38 years that the unit would serve in the UK.

The first aircraft, a brand new F Mk 6 XS928 was collected from Warton by the Squadron's CO, Sqn Ldr Peter Collins on 4th April with three more on strength by the end of the month. As with No.5 Squadron, most of the pilots already had Lightning experience and during a no notice TACEVAL (Tactical Evaluation) called on 26th April, all of the squadron's pilots flew in aircraft of Nos.23 and 74 Squadrons, as their own aircraft were still undergoing acceptance checks. A slow down in the delivery of new aircraft was eased by the acquisition in May of T Mk 5 XS416 from No.74 Squadron. Although not yet operational, the squadron held a thirty-six hour period of QRA on behalf of No.23 Squadron, who were temporarily stood down to celebrate the award of the Dacre Trophy.

)11 SQUADRON

No.11 Squadron was re-formed at Leuchars on 3rd April 1967 to fill a gap that was soon to be created in Britain's most northerly Air Defence region due to No.74 Squadron's departure to Singapore.

The squadron was declared operational at the end of May, and by 3rd July they had received their full complement of aircraft with the collection of XS934. Four aircraft took part in the squadron's first exchange visit, detaching to the RDAF base at Skrydstrup between 11th and 14th August. For the forthcoming Battle of Britain at Home Day the squadron practiced a four-ship formation and a solo aerobatics sequence and displayed at Acklington and Leuchars on 16th September.

At the end of October the squadron began in-flight refuelling training, with some of their aircraft fitted with the over-wing tanks. Two aircraft so configured, took part in an endurance trial on 29th November and although one aircraft experienced refuelling problems, the other completed a successful eight-hour sortie without incident.

Handing over their Northern QRA commitments to No.5 Squadron during their absence, No.11 Squadron deployed six aircraft to RAF Valley on 1st February 1968 for their first Armament Practice Camp.

Non-operational events for the year saw four of their aircraft included in the flypast during HRH The Queen's Review of the RAF at Abingdon, with an additional aircraft provided for the static display. A further eight aircraft flew in a sixteen Lightning formation over St. Andrews on 22nd August, the day Leuchars was conferred with the Freedom of the City.

The end of the year saw the squadron heavily engaged in a massive engineering programme that necessitated most of their aircraft requiring engine changes and then preparations were begun for exercise 'Piscator Plus'. This was to be the largest air-to-air refuelling exercise so far undertaken by the RAF with ten of No.11 Squadron's Lightnings, supported by sixteen Victor tankers drawn from Nos.55, 57 and 214 Squadrons, deployed to Tengah, Singapore, a distance of 9,180 miles. The first aircraft departing in pairs, left Leuchars on 6th January, with all aircraft staging through Muhurraq and Gan, arriving at Tengah on 11th January after a total of 18 flying hours.

The four-week visit to the Far East was designed to demonstrate and test Strike Command's capability to reinforce the air defence of the Singapore bases. Taking part in a number of exercises, two aircraft also undertook a short visit to RAAF Butterworth.

April 1970 saw the squadron's involvement in an intense period of QRA activity as between 15th and 24th of the month, forty Soviet long-range aircraft, mostly Bears and Badgers, were intercepted and identified from a total of forty-one scrambles.

Now well established at Leuchars, No.43 Squadron and the longer range Phantom FG Mk 1 were increasingly taking over Northern QRA responsibilities and No.11 Squadron were relocated to Binbrook, leaving No.23 Squadron as the last remaining Lightning squadron at this Scottish base. The first aircraft arrived at Binbrook on 22nd March 1972, heralding a partnership with No.5 Squadron that was to last for sixteen years.

Both squadrons' histories now ran more or less parallel courses at Binbrook with one major exception. With the run-down of the Lightning Force beginning and the disbandment of its main training infrastructure, No.226 OCU in September 1974, No.11 Squadron were tasked with the training of new pilots and providing refresher courses for others returning to flying the type. To fulfil these duties, the squadron was enlarged with the addition of a small number of the former OCU's T Mk 5 aircraft into 'C' Flight. They retained this task for a year, when the role was handed over to the newly formed Lightning Training Flight (LTF) at Binbrook in October 1975.

Destined to be the last of the RAF's Lightning squadrons, following the disbandment of No.5 Squadron in December 1987, No.11 Squadron entered into their final few months. Maintaining their full operational commitment they conducted their final Missile Practice Camp at RAF Valley. These last few months also saw a number of their Lightnings fitted with overwing tanks and used in conjunction with British Aerospace on the Tornado F Mk 3 trials programme. In fact the Tornado's protracted entry into service was the prime reason for the Lightning's extended service.

Below: A pair of 11 Squadron's F Mk 6s stand alert in Binbrook's 'Battle hangar' in the summer of 1974.

With a final nine-ship formation flown on 29th April 1988, No.11 Squadron disbanded. The pilots' final duties in May were the delivery of their former aircraft to airfields around the UK and overseas, for Battle Damage Repair Training or preservation.

On 30th June 1988, Sqn Ldr J Aldington had the distinction of making the RAF's final Lightning flight, when he delivered XS923 to Cranfield, ending an era.

11 SQUADRON

Previously flew:
Gloster Javelin FAW Mk 9s from December 1962.

Lightnings:
F Mk 6s from 4th April 1967.

Bases:
Leuchars, Scotland, from 1st April 1967
Binbrook, Lincolnshire, from 22nd March 1972.

Disbanded:
29th April 1988.

Later:
Panavia Tornados at Leeming, Yorkshire, from 30th June 1988, to date.

Badge:
Two eagles volant in pale.
Motto: Ociores acrierosque aquilis –
Swifter and keener than eagles.

No.11 Squadron re-formed at Leuchars on 1st April 1967 to fill the Air Defence gap created by No.74 Squadron's departure to Singapore. Photographed at Finningley, Lightning F Mk 6, XR757/D displays the squadron's original tail badge marking of two brown eagles on a white disc.

With the arrival of the longer range Phantom FG Mk 1s at Leuchars, No.11 Squadron relocated to Binbrook on 22nd March 1972. A highly polished Lightning F Mk 6, XS904/A, with matching over-wing tanks, was photographed at Binbrook in July 1972. The white-painted section of fuselage spine to keep the AVPIN tank cool is prominent.

Lightning F Mk 6, XR769/J taxis in at Leconfield following an August 1973 thunderstorm. This aircraft went on to achieve 4,070 flying hours before becoming the RAF's last Lightning loss when it crashed into the North Sea following an engine fire on 11th April 1988. The pilot ejected safely.

After a very tight circuit, Lightning F Mk 6, XR765/C, levels out moments before touchdown at Leconfield in June 1976.

Opposite page top: Having spent the previous two years in storage, Lightning F Mk 3, XP737/P, photographed at Leconfield in July 1976, was received by No.11 Squadron in pristine condition in May of the same year.

Opposite page bottom: Photographed during the transition from natural metal finish to grey and green camouflage, Lightning F Mk 6s, XR763/B and XR757/D get airborne from Leconfield on a stormy April 1976 afternoon.
D Hemingway

One day they were 'silver', the next day camouflaged. Lightning F Mk 6, XS936/G, had its squadron markings re-applied in stages between sorties. Photographed at Leconfield in the summer of 1976, it awaits the black eagles to be painted on to the fin and the completion of the nose markings.

A brief six months service period with No.11 Squadron ended on 30th July 1976 for Lightning F Mk 6, XS937/K when it was abandoned off Flamborough Head due to the starboard undercarriage leg not being able to lock down. The pilot ejected safely. The aircraft was photographed 'burning rubber' on Leconfield's runway just days before its unfortunate loss.

One of a small number of Binbrook Lightnings painted in an experimental overall Dark Green upper surface scheme, Lightning T Mk 5, XS452/T, was photographed on Binbrook's ASP in August 1977. At the time of writing, this Lightning still lives on and flies, in South Africa, registered as ZU-BDD. It resides at Thunder Valley marked up as 'BT' of No.11 Squadron, its last owner, but now flaunts an overall gloss black colour scheme!

XS901/G with its short-lived adhesive day-glo panels across the fin. It also carries a Luftwaffe WS 10 unit 'zap' on its nose as a memento of an exchange visit to Jever from where it had returned just a few days previously.

Lightning F Mk 6s, XR727/F and XS901/G, were specially marked with adhesive day-glo panels to represent the aircraft as 'bandits' for a set piece air display during Binbrook's August 1978 Open Day.

Photographed in its element, XS923/BE, was one of several F Mk 6s to retain the Dark Green/Dark Sea Grey upper surface camouflage scheme to the bitter end. This aircraft had the distinction of flying the RAF's last Lightning sortie, when it was delivered to its new owner, Mr Arnold Glass at Cranfield, on 30th June 1988. *NWHG Warton*

Opposite page top: A stark contrast of shades of grey and colour demarcations on No.11 Squadron's flight line in July 1982. Lightning F Mk 3, XR749/BM, in the foreground, had served with every unit in the Binbrook Wing since 1972, amassing some 2,542 flying hours. Since retirement in February 1987, it has resided at several private locations in the north of England. It was last heard of in Peterhead in 2003.

Opposite page bottom: Lightning F Mk 6, XS933 photographed whilst being re-fuelled during a series of quick turn around sorties at Binbrook in July 1984.

With its dark grey camouflage blending in with the stormy sky, XS919 has its braking parachute re-packed on Binbrook's ASP in August 1985.

Wg Cdr Jake Jarron, in F Mk 6, XS903/BA, leads the way back to dispersal after No.11 Squadron's last nine ship formation flight on 29th April 1988, formally ending the RAF's Lightning era. This aircraft's final flight, on 18th May 1988, was to Elvington, where the aircraft is now preserved by the Yorkshire Air Museum. Both fin and fuselage spine are painted black.

Having been the all-weather fighter defence component of the Near East Air Force (NEAF) since 1963, based at Nicosia and then Akrotiri in Cyprus, No.29 Squadron were relieved of their role by the arrival of No.56 Squadron with their Lightnings in April 1967, and they then returned to Wattisham. With the disposal of their former Javelins, a new No.29 Squadron re-formed on 10th May. The nucleus of the squadron had commenced flying immediately after No.56 Squadron's departure with a pair of Lightning F Mk 3s, XP765 and XP698, left behind by the squadron, and the only new aircraft that they were to receive, T Mk 5 XV328.

X29 SQUADRON

No.29 Squadron was the last of the planned nine squadrons that were to make up the Lightning Force and subsequently were also to operate this aircraft for the shortest period of time.

Joined by a third F Mk 3, XP694, which had been retained at Warton for trials work and was consequently a low hours airframe, the squadron began a varied flying programme helped by the fact that all of the initial pilots and ground crew were Lightning experienced, having been transferred from both Nos.56 and 11 Squadrons.

The squadron soon took part in their first exercise, Fighter Command's annual *Kingpin*, called on 6th July, for which the engineers produced a 100% serviceability rate. The same could not be said for some of the 'second-hand' Lightnings that were still being received, with a mammoth engineering task being necessary to bring them up to the required modification state.

Despite still having only six serviceable aircraft, No.29 Squadron were declared operational on 16th August 1967, just two months after reforming. On 15th September they took over the Southern QRA commitment from co-located No.111 Squadron, who had been temporarily despatched to Leuchars. With the squadrons resources stretched to maintain the pair

of aircraft on alert, plus two pre-requisite back up aircraft, normal operational training was severely curtailed.

The squadron were able to deploy on their first exchange visit later in the month when three F Mk 3s and the T Mk 5 were flown to the Royal Norwegian Air Force base at Oerland on the 29th. Then October saw their involvement as the sole Lightning squadron participating in exercise *Co-op*, and they ended their first year of flying during exercise *Ricochet* called on 29th December.

On 2nd March 1968, the squadron detached six of their Lightnings to RAF Valley for their first Missile Practice Camp, successfully firing four Red Top rounds during their visit. Another milestone for them was the ability to generate twelve of their aircraft to contribute to a Wattisham Wing flypast over Ipswich on 4th April to celebrate the 50th Anniversary of the formation of the RAF. Later in the month, aircraft of each of Fighter Command's squadrons gathered at Wattisham to prepare for the Commands merger with Bomber Command into Strike Command. No.29 Squadron contributed three of its aircraft for the farewell flypast, flown on 25th April.

In July, No.29 Squadron sent a five aircraft detachment on a ten-day goodwill visit to the Italian Air Force base at Grosseto, this being the first exchange between the two countries since the end of the Second World War.

A scheduled deployment to Cyprus in June was postponed because of a strike by French Air Traffic Controllers but eventually got underway on 30th September, with six aircraft departing for Nicosia, as Akrotiri's runways were under repair at that time.

April 14th 1969, saw the squadron's deployment of ten aircraft to Luqa and its participation in the Malta Air Defence exercise during the second week in May. Taking advantage of Malta's fine weather, No.29 Squadron began to work up a four-ship formation team in preparation for a visit by HRH Princess Margaret back at Wattisham on 4th July. With runway resurfacing due to start at Wattisham at the end of July, No.29 Squadron departed to Coltishall until they re-located to Binbrook in September. The squadron took over QRA from resident No.5 Squadron on 24th September for a month, finally returning to Wattisham in time for Christmas.

The squadron suffered their first aircraft loss on 25th January 1971, when an engine fire and subsequent loss of control forced its USAF exchange visit pilot to eject from XP756 during a night time sortie. After spending an uncomfortable two hours in the North Sea, the pilot was rescued by a USAF helicopter. The loss of XP705 followed in July whilst on a Cyprus detachment, forcing the pilot to eject following a double re-heat fire. This second loss was the cause of particular concern as it had only recently completed the latest round of fire integrity modifications. The remaining aircraft were grounded for several days for checks and rectification work before resuming their flying programme. A third and disastrous loss for the squadron occurred on 22nd September, when XP736 and its pilot were lost during a supersonic interception practice over the North Sea, with neither the pilot nor the wreckage being found.

No.29 Squadron's ill fortune continued in 1972 with the loss of three more aircraft, two of which, XP698 and 747, collided over the North Sea on February 16th with only one pilot surviving. XP700 was lost on 7th August when it sank back onto the runway after undercarriage retraction. The aircraft skidded on its belly for over 500 yards before becoming airborne again; the pilot ejecting safely after reaching 3,000 ft.

Below: The only new built Lightning delivered to 29 Squadron was T Mk 5 XV328. seen here visiting Binbrook in April 1971.

On a much lighter note, the beginning of September was spent working up a routine for the forthcoming Battle of Britain display to be held at Wattisham on September 16th.

The squadron continued its schedule of activities into 1974, when it won the Dacre Trophy, presented to the No.11 Group squadron judged to be the most proficient in all aspects of fighter operations. After little more than seven years with the Lightnings No.29 Squadron disbanded as the last Lightning F Mk 3 user and handed over its 'number plate' to its Phantom FGR Mk 2-equipped successor on 31st December 1974.

29 SQUADRON

Previously flew:
Gloster Javelin F(AW) Mk 9s from April 1961.

Lightnings:
F Mk 3s from 10th May 1967.

Bases:
Wattisham, Suffolk, throughout.

Disbanded:
31st December 1974.

Later:
McDonnell-Douglas Phantom FGR Mk 2s from January 1975; Panavia Tornado F Mk 3s from April 1987. Preparing to become the Eurofighter Typhoon Operational Conversion Unit at Coningsby, Lincolnshire.

Badge:
An eagle in flight, preying on a buzzard.
Motto: Impiger et acer - Energetic and keen.

Top: The last frontline squadron to receive the Lightning - and to fly it for the shortest time - was No.29 Squadron, which formed at Wattisham on 10th May 1967. Equipped with F Mk 3s, the unit filled the void in the UK's southern air defence region, left by the departure of No.56 Squadron to Cyprus. Lightning F Mk 3, XP705/L photographed at Finningley in September 1969, was lost in the Mediterranean following a re-heat fire in July 1971. The pilot ejected safely.

Above: Although receiving their F Mk 3s as 'hand-me-downs', mainly from Nos.23 and 74 Squadrons, XP694/D only had short periods of use by the A&AEE and BAC Warton before being delivered to No.29 Squadron with just 97 hours on the clock. Surviving longer than many of its sister F Mk 3s, it was passed on to the Binbrook Wing in 1975 and served there until mid-1984 before finally 'expiring' on the Otterburn ranges. *D Hemingway*

Originally coded 'F' when first received by the squadron, XP708, now re-coded 'N', was photographed on No.29 Squadron's flight line at Wattisham in June 1974.
G *Kipp*

Lightning F Mk 3, XP765/A, armed with white-finned Red Top air-to-air missiles was captured on camera at Wattisham's last Battle of Britain Air Show, in September 1972. XP765 had previously served with No.56 Squadron.
D *Hemingway*

Opposite page top: The very last Lightning from the F Mk 3 batch, XR751 was placed on the F Mk 6 conversion programme at Warton before the contract was amended and it was re-converted back to its original form. It was then delivered to No.226 OCU and then from April 1971 served a mere eighteen months with No.29 Squadron as 'Q', before joining the Binbrook Wing in November 1972. *D Hemingway*

Opposite page bottom: A neat formation by three Lightning F Mk 3s, XP765/A, XP743/B and XP694/D, displaying at Wattisham's 1972 Air Show. XP765 and XP694 are carrying Red Top air-to-air missiles whilst XP743 has Firestreaks. *D Hemingway*

Whereas 111 Squadrons F Mk 3s were scrapped in situ at Wattisham, 60 MU at Leconfield were tasked with the spares reclamation of 29 Squadrons F Mk 3s before they were dumped on the airfield. The Lightning was never over endowed with access panels, most of which can be seen removed in this September 1975 photograph. *D Hemingway*

Last minute salvaging on XP755/E before being dumped on its belly at No.60 MU Leconfield in September 1975.

TRAINING AND SECOND LINE UNITS

With the development of the English Electric P.1 into a viable weapons system gathering pace, plans were formulated as early as 1957 for the pilots who would one day fly this Mach 2 interceptor.

Formed at Coltishall on 4th January 1960 with the support of the Central Fighter Establishment, the Lightning Conversion Unit began conversion training by using borrowed aircraft from the AFDS and a Lightning F Mk 1 simulator, as no two-seat Lightnings would be available for some time.

Initially, only jet pilots with a minimum 1,000 hours experience were chosen to fly the new fighter. The syllabus began with a five-day course on aviation medicine at RAF Upwood, followed by seven days of lectures associated with the aircrafts' systems and emergency drills. Training continued with ten one-hour sorties on the simulator before a first solo flight in the F Mk 1 itself, accompanied by an instructor in a Hunter T Mk 7 chase plane. Transition to the Lightning, with over twice the performance of their former Hunters or Javelins was accomplished by the pilots with relative ease and enabled the first squadron to begin its work up on the type in June 1960.

With a change of name to the Lightning Conversion Squadron, and a move north to Middleton St.George, they continued their training task with borrowed aircraft until the arrival of their first T Mk 4, XM970, on 16th June 1962. A gradual build up of two-seaters was complemented by seven ex-No.74 Squadron F Mk 1s in 1963 at the same time as another change of title to No.226 Operational Conversion Unit, with a shadow identity as No.145 Squadron. With Mid-dleton St.George now transformed into a Lightning base, the airfield was eventually sold for civilian use to become Teesside Airport. No.226 OCU and their fourteen aircraft moved yet again, this time to a more permanent home at Coltishall on 14th April 1964.

With the arrival of their first T Mk 5 on 20th April 1965, No.226 OCU also began to replace its F Mk 1 aircraft with F Mk 1A models, now redundant from Nos.56 and 111 Squadrons. By the end of the 1960s, the unit establishment had risen to around thirty-six aircraft to which were added a number of F Mk 3s, from June 1970.

From early May 1971, No.226 OCU's three squadrons were given a change of identity with No.1 Squadron (The Conversion Squadron) and No.2 Squadron (The Weapons Squadron) adopting No.65 Squadron's 'shadow' identity and markings for their F Mk 1As and T Mk 4s. No.3 (The Advanced Squadron) became No.2T Squadron with their F Mk 3 and T Mk 5s, receiving new markings of light blue and white triangles flanking the nose roundel and a stylised '2T' tail badge.

Although never called upon to fulfil their 'shadow role' in any political emergency, No.226 OCU's aircraft and occasionally their instructors, were frequently borrowed to make up deficiencies in the squadrons due to aircraft undergoing major servicing or modifications.

With the rundown of the Lightning Force imminent, No.65 Squadron disbanded on 31st July 1974, with No.2T Squadron following suit at the end of September. The pilot training role, for what was foreseen to be only a handful of years, was handed over to No.11 Squadron's 'C' Flight at Binbrook.

LIGHTNING TRAINING FLIGHT

With it becoming apparent that the Lightning's successor, the Tornado ADV, was still several years away, No.11 Squadron's training task at Binbrook was taken over by the Lightning Training Flight, formed in September 1975. With a unit establishment of four each of the T Mk 5 and F Mk 3 variants, the training pattern was essentially the same as that of No.226 OCU, with the new pilots having first gained fast jet experience at one of the Tactical Weapons Units flying the Hawk T Mk 1. Training began with two weeks of ground school, followed by several sorties in the simulator. Actual conversion to the Lightning began with five sorties in a T Mk 5 before the first solo flight in a F Mk 3. In 1979 a F Mk 6 was added to the LTF fleet to give the new pilot a 'feel' for this much heavier variant, before his posting to either of Binbrook's squadrons.

The LTF also maintained one or two aircraft at a time for

the purpose of supplementing the two squadrons' aircraft and pilot strength in times of exercise, under the banner Lightning Augmentation Flight, between 1980-1983. After 12 years of service, and the Lightning era now rapidly drawing to a close, the LTF completed its final course in April 1987.

AIR FIGHTING DEVELOPMENT SQUADRON

Itself a component of the Central Fighter Establishment, the Air Fighting Development Squadron (AFDS) became the first service operator of the Lightning when it received its first aircraft in December 1959 followed by two more in February and March 1960. These were received from the pre-production development batch at Coltishall. The AFDS was tasked with the evaluation of the aircraft and development of operational tactics prior to the type entering service.

From the delivery of the first full production standard F Mk 1, XM135 in May 1960, every mark of Lightning, with the exception of the F Mk 2A variant, was evaluated, with the squadron usually receiving two or three examples of each mark for the purpose. Re-named the Fighter Command Trials Unit (FCTU) in February 1966, one of their ultimate tasks was the evaluation of two F Mk 1s modified for the target facilities role, with the unit finally disbanding in June 1967.

Below: T Mk 4 XM972 of 226 OCU leads out a five-ship formation team at Leconfield's July 1968 Air Show.

TARGET FACILITIES FLIGHT

Upon the Lightning's entry into squadron service, realistic supersonic and high-flying targets were limited to the co-operation and availability of USAF aircraft such as the limited number of Century Series (i.e. F-100 and F-104) aircraft deployed in Europe for interception training. The use of their own Lightning aircraft, particularly in the early years was a drain on the squadron's resources with serviceability problems and modification programmes frequently depleting the numbers of their aircraft available to meet their normal tasks.

After the withdrawal of the F Mk 1 and F Mk 1A models from squadron service, a number of them were overhauled, stripped of their cannon armament, and had their AI radar replaced with a Luneberg Lens which increased the aircrafts radar reflection. Thus modified and trialled by the FCTU, these aircraft were issued to each of the UK's Lightning Wings at Binbrook, Leuchars and Wattisham in 1966.

Each flight usually operated with three aircraft as an autonomous unit, each devising their own individual unit markings with a fin badge based on its station's crest. All three TFFs were disbanded on 31st December 1973, as an economy measure deemed necessary to avoid the provision of F Mk 1 spares at the bases involved. In 1974, each of the F Mk 6 squadrons were issued with three F Mk 3s which as well as fulfilling the squadron's operational role, were also utilised in the target role for practice interceptions.

Top: The Lightning Conversion Unit (LCU) was formed at Coltishall on 4th January 1960, but did not receive their first aircraft, a T Mk 4, XM970, until 27th June 1962, after their move to Middleton St George. Returning to Coltishall on13th April 1964 XM970 was photographed there in September 1969, six years after the unit had been re-named No.226 OCU. *D Hemingway*

Above: On becoming No.226 OCU, in keeping with the front line operational squadrons, the 'T-Birds' and newly acquired F Mk 1s, were adorned with these scarlet and white markings that were based on the colours of St George. This Lightning F Mk 1, XM146 was photographed circa 1964. *R Lindsay*

TRAINING AND SECOND LINE UNITS

Top: On the standardisation of Fighter Command's colour schemes in 1966, their previous colourful scheme was replaced with the markings of No.226 OCU's shadow identity, No.145 Squadron. Photographed whilst awaiting its allocated display slot at Leconfield's July 1968 Air Show, Lightning T Mk 4 XM972 served its entire service life with the OCU.

Above: Lightning T Mk 5s began to supplement the T Mk 4s in April 1965. XS420, armed with Red Top AAMs, was photographed at Coltishall in September 1969. *D Hemingway*

Top: Lightning T Mk 5, XS449 blasts off from Lakenheath's runway in June 1970, to give the 48th TFW and assembled air show crowd a splendid display of the Lightning T-Bird's amazing agility.

Above: In the late 1960s, the OCU strength peaked at around thirty-six aircraft and its three component squadrons were given stronger identities. No.1 Squadron OCU, tasked with Conversion Training, operated the T Mk 4 and F Mk 1A, and adopted No.65 Squadron as its shadow identity, as seen here on F Mk 1A XM182, photographed in August 1972.

Lightning F Mk 1A, XM189 demonstrates its phenomenal rate of climb at Upper Heyford in August 1972. No.2 Squadron of the OCU also used No.65 Shadow Squadron aircraft for weapons training. Note the Firestreak AAMs in place.

Opposite page top: No.3 Squadron OCU, the Advanced Squadron, adopted its new identity as 2T Squadron, with pale blue chevrons flanking the nose roundel and a stylised '2T' tail badge marking. Photographed at Binbrook in July 1972, this Lightning F Mk 3, XP707, met its demise at the Lincolnshire base fifteen years later, on 19th March 1987, whilst practising for a display routine. Fortunately its LTF pilot ejected successfully from a very low level.

Opposite page bottom: Lightning F Mk 3, XP737 was the Lightning display aircraft for 1973, and was photographed here at Lakenheath in July of that year. The 2T marking is carried on the fin and the Red Top AAMs are rather gaudily painted.

Lightning F Mk 3, XR716 makes a fast 'run through' at the beginning of its display during Leconfield's 1974 Open Day. Typical for this mark is the bright glint off the straight leading edge wings and the carriage of Red Top AAMs.

Lightning T Mk 5, XS423 returns to a wet Leconfield in the summer of 1973 whilst on short term loan to Nos.5 and 11 Squadrons, based at RAF Binbrook. The stylised '2T' tail badge marking and the pale blue chevrons flanking the nose roundel are well illustrated in this photograph.

A Red Top armed Lightning T Mk 5, XS454, crosses Leconfield's overshoot area when landing for a fuel stop in August 1973. Red Top AAMs are fitted.

Flown by Flt Lt Pete Chapman, for the 1974 display season, Lightning F Mk 3, XP696, was specially painted with a white fin and spine. This photograph was probably taken at the aircraft's final display of that year, at Finningley, with the OCU disbanding soon afterwards.

Opposite page top: The Lightning Training Flight formed at Binbrook in October 1975 as a successor to C Flight of No.11 Squadron, to continue the training of Lightning pilots following the disbandment of No.226 OCU. The normal establishment was four each of Lightning T Mk 5s and F.3s with an F Mk 6 added in 1979. Lightning T Mk 5 XS451 was photographed here in April 1976, operating out of Coningsby, whilst runway repairs were carried out at Binbrook.

Opposite page bottom: Displayed at Alconbury in August 1980, Lightning F Mk 3 XR751 still shows traces of its representative No.111 Squadron markings on the nose, which were applied for Binbrook's 25th Anniversary of the Lightning celebrations.

Opposite page top: Signalling the end of the natural metal era, Lightning T Mk 5, XS458/Z was painted an experimental dark grey scheme at Binbrook in late 1975. This aircraft still survives in excellent condition at Cranfield, Bedfordshire and in 2004 was decorated in special markings to celebrate the 50th Anniversary of the Lightning's first flight.

Opposite page bottom: Resplendent in the brighter of the various grey schemes applied to the Lightnings in their final years, XS419/DV basks in the Binbrook sun in July 1982.

Starboard side view of Lightning T Mk 5, XS419/DV, (seen on the previous page), taxiing out to begin a July 1982 sortie at Binbrook. The red star on the fin was applied to denote this aircraft as an Eastern Bloc defector during a recent exercise.

With one burner fully lit and the second igniting, XS458 is starting a fast taxi run at Cranfield in 1996, where it is preserved but not allowed to fly. *NWHG Warton*

Opposite page top: Typical of the Lightning F Mk 6s operated by the LTF, XS895/DF, is fitted with the all-fuel ventral tank to give it maximum endurance for training flights.

Opposite page bottom: Lightning F Mk 6, XR757/BE, sporting an No.11 Squadron code whilst also displaying the Lightning Augmentation Flight's small day-glow badge on its fin at Binbrook in August 1982.

Above: Maintained by the LTF, the Lightning Augmentation Flight held a small number of both F Mk 3 and F Mk 6 Lightnings to supplement the operational squadrons' strength and provide aircraft for refresher courses. F Mk 3, XP694 was photographed in April 1982.

A superb formation led by Station Commander Gp Cpt John Spencer's individually coded
Lightning F Mk 6, XR728/JS, still bearing the now disbanded LTF badge. Light grey painted T Mk
5, XS452/BT, is in the centre, with the Dark Sea Grey/Dark Green F Mk 6, XS923/BE, with the
old 'large' No 11 Squadron twin eagles badge on the fin in the background. *NWHG Warton*

Top: The Air Fighting Development Squadron, a component of the Central Fighter Establishment was tasked with the introduction of the Lightning into RAF service. Photographed at Finningley in September 1961, Lightning F Mk 1, XM136/E, is seen here being towed to the runway to give a short flying display.

Above: Another view of Lightning F Mk 1, XM136/E, being towed to Finningley's runway in September 1961, displays the red and black horizontally striped bars either side of the nose roundel and the Air Fighting Development Squadron badge on the fin.

Top: The Air Fighting Development Squadron operated every variant of the Lightning with the exception of the F Mk 2A until it disbanded in 1965. Here F Mk 2, XN726/K, with revised AFDS fin markings taxis in at Binbrook circa summer 1963. *via D Tuplin*

Above: A number of surplus Lightning F Mk 1 and F Mk 1A aircraft were converted for Target Facilities duties and served with the squadrons and as autonomous units at different times from 1966 until 1973. Lightning F Mk 1A, XM173, photographed in June 1973, was one of three F Mk 1A's operated by the Binbrook TFF.

Stripped of most of their operational equipment, the Target Facilities Flight Lightnings had their AI 23 radar removed and replaced with a Luneberg Lens, increasing the aircraft's radar reflection for the benefit of trainee Lightning pilots on their sorties. Lightning F Mk 1A, XM183, of the Binbrook TFF, was photographed on its return to Leconfield in May 1973.

Resplendent in its 'Royal Scottish Air Force' markings, Lightning F Mk 1A, XM173 was only operated by the Leuchars TFF for three months, from December 1971 to March 1972, when it was seen here on approach to Leconfield. It served next with Binbrook's TFF until being relegated to ground instructional use and was finally transported to RAF Bentley Priory to be displayed there in November 1976.

Top: The subject of the dramatic night time reheat shot on page 11, Lightning F Mk 1, XM145, ex-Leuchars TFF, languishes on Leconfield's dump in July 1974, after only 876 flying hours. *D Hemingway*

Above: Lightning F Mk 1, XM139 of the Wattisham TFF was the display aircraft for the 1970-71 season. It is seen here at Upper Heyford in June, flown by Flt Lt Russ Pengelly and wearing its 1971 Paris Air Salon number.

Normally unarmed for TFF duties, missiles were only carried for aerobatic displays, giving the aircraft better handling characteristics. Lightning F Mk 1A, XM177, of the Wattisham TFF, displayed at Bentwaters on a sunny day in May 1971.

Still bearing Leuchars TFF fin badge, the last flying days of XM135 were spent with No.60 MU Leconfield, being used as a continuation trainer by the resident test pilot. This aircraft was flown to the Imperial War Museum at Duxford on 20th November 1974 and is now on show in No.74 Squadron colours.

Lightning T Mk 4 XM970 also served as a continuation trainer at No.60 MU from July 1974 to January 1976 when it was passed on to No.19 Squadron in Germany. It was photographed returning to Leconfield in the late afternoon sunshine of October 1975.

Originally built as the first production Lightning F Mk 3, XP693 seen here, and XP697, were retained by BAC and used for the development flying of the extended range development that was to be designated as the F Mk 6. XP693 was photographed at 56 Squadron's (Phantom) disbandment display at Wattisham in July 1992.

Opposite page top and bottom: After being phased out of RAF service, three ex-Binbrook F Mk 6s were flown to BAe Warton for use on Tornado radar trials, flying until 1992. The three Lightnings, XR724, XS904 and XS928, were usually flown configured with over wing tanks to increase their endurance. After being placed on Warton's dump, XS928 has now been restored and is on display outside their Flight Test Centre.
NWHG Warton

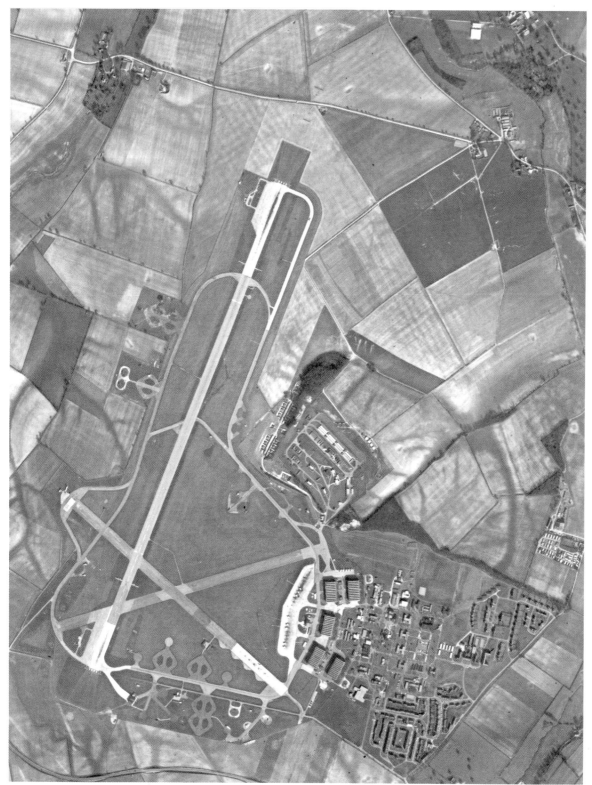

GLOSSARY

AAM	Air to Air Missile
A&AEE	Aeroplane & Armament Experimental Establishment
ADV	Air Defence Variant
AFCENT	Air Forces Central (Europe)
AFDS	Air Fighting Development Squadron
AI	Airborne Interception
ASTOR	Airborne Stand-Off Radar
AVPIN	Isopropyl Nitrate
BAC	British Aircraft Corporation
CO	Commanding Officer
FCTU	Fighter Command Trials Unit
FEAF	Far East Air Force
Flt Lt	Flight Lieutenant
FOD	Foreign Object Damage
IFR	In-flight Refuelling
LCU	Lightning Conversion Unit
LOX	Liquid Oxygen
LTF	Lightning Training Flight
MiG	Mikoyan-Gurevich
MU	Maintenance Unit
NATO	North Atlantic Treaty Organisation
NEAF	Near East Air Force
NWHG	North West Heritage Group
OCU	Operational Conversion Unit
QRA	Quick Reaction Alert. Later became Intercepter Alert Force. (IAF)
RAAF	Royal Australian Air Force
RDAF	Royal Danish Air Force
RJAF	Royal Jordanian Air Force
RNorAF	Royal Norwegian Air Force
SBAC	Society of British Aerospace Companies
Sqn Ldr	Squadron Leader
TACEVAL	Tactical Evaluation
TFF	Target Facilities Flight
TFS	Tactical Fighter Squadron
TFW	Tactical Fighter Wing
Tu	Tupolev

Aircraft Designations

AEW	Airborne Early Warning
F	Fighter
FAW	Fighter All Weather
FG	Fighter Ground Attack
FGR	Fighter Ground Attack and Reconnaissance
KC	Tanker Transport
R	Reconnaissance
T	Trainer

RAF Binbrook basks in the heat of the summer of 1976 with nine operational Lightnings parked on the ASP. A single aircraft can be seen taxiing for take off while at least thirteen life expired airframes are scattered around the airfield.
via Martyn Chorlton